# MAXIMILIEN ROBESPIERRE

# MAXIMILIEN ROBESPIERRE

S. L. Carson

CHELSEA HOUSE PUBLISHERS
NEW YORK
NEW HAVEN     PHILADELPHIA

EDITOR-IN-CHIEF: Nancy Toff
EXECUTIVE EDITOR: Remmel T. Nunn
MANAGING EDITOR: Karyn Gullen Browne
COPY CHIEF: Juliann Barbato
PICTURE EDITOR: Adrian G. Allen
ART DIRECTOR: Giannella Garrett
MANUFACTURING MANAGER: Gerald Levine

*Staff for* MAXIMILIEN ROBESPIERRE:

SENIOR EDITOR: John W. Selfridge
ASSISTANT EDITOR: Bert Yaeger
EDITORIAL ASSISTANT: James Guiry
COPY EDITOR: Michael Goodman
PICTURE RESEARCHER: Juliette Dickstein
SENIOR DESIGNER: David Murray
ASSISTANT DESIGNER: Jill Goldreyer
DESIGNERS: Laura Lang, Donna Sinisgalli
PRODUCTION COORDINATOR: Laura McCormick
COVER ILLUSTRATION: Mark Sparacio

CREATIVE DIRECTOR: Harold Steinberg

1 3 5 7 9 8 6 4 2

Library of Congress Cataloging in Publication Data

Carson, S. L. MAXIMILIEN ROBESPIERRE

(World leaders past & present)
Bibliography: p.
Includes index.
1. Robespierre, Maximilien, 1758–1794—Juvenile literature.
2. Revolutionists—France—Biography—Juvenile literature.
3. France—History—Revolution, 1789–1794—Juvenile
literature. [1. Robespierre, Maximilien, 1758–1794.
2. Revolutionists. 3. France—History—Revolution,
1789–1794] I. Title.  II. Series: World leaders past &
present.
DC146.R6C28     1988     944.04′1′0924 [92]  87-13237

ISBN 0-87754-549-9

# Contents

ADENAUER
ALEXANDER THE GREAT
MARC ANTONY
KING ARTHUR
ATATÜRK
ATTLEE
BEGIN
BEN-GURION
BISMARCK
LÉON BLUM
BOLÍVAR
CESARE BORGIA
BRANDT
BREZHNEV
CAESAR
CALVIN
CASTRO
CATHERINE THE GREAT
CHARLEMAGNE
CHIANG KAI-SHEK
CHURCHILL
CLEMENCEAU
CLEOPATRA
CORTÉS
CROMWELL
DANTON
DE GAULLE
DE VALERA
DISRAELI
EISENHOWER
ELEANOR OF AQUITAINE
QUEEN ELIZABETH I
FERDINAND AND ISABELLA
FRANCO

FREDERICK THE GREAT
INDIRA GANDHI
MOHANDAS GANDHI
GARIBALDI
GENGHIS KHAN
GLADSTONE
GORBACHEV
HAMMARSKJÖLD
HENRY VIII
HENRY OF NAVARRE
HINDENBURG
HITLER
HO CHI MINH
HUSSEIN
IVAN THE TERRIBLE
ANDREW JACKSON
JEFFERSON
JOAN OF ARC
POPE JOHN XXIII
LYNDON JOHNSON
JUÁREZ
JOHN F. KENNEDY
KENYATTA
KHOMEINI
KHRUSHCHEV
MARTIN LUTHER KING, JR.
KISSINGER
LENIN
LINCOLN
LLOYD GEORGE
LOUIS XIV
LUTHER
JUDAS MACCABEUS
MAO ZEDONG

MARY, QUEEN OF SCOTS
GOLDA MEIR
METTERNICH
MUSSOLINI
NAPOLEON
NASSER
NEHRU
NERO
NICHOLAS II
NIXON
NKRUMAH
PERICLES
PERÓN
QADDAFI
ROBESPIERRE
ELEANOR ROOSEVELT
FRANKLIN D. ROOSEVELT
THEODORE ROOSEVELT
SADAT
STALIN
SUN YAT-SEN
TAMERLANE
THATCHER
TITO
TROTSKY
TRUDEAU
TRUMAN
VICTORIA
WASHINGTON
WEIZMANN
WOODROW WILSON
XERXES
ZHOU ENLAI

# ON LEADERSHIP
## Arthur M. Schlesinger, jr.

LEADERSHIP, it may be said, is really what makes the world go round. Love no doubt smooths the passage; but love is a private transaction between consenting adults. Leadership is a public transaction with history. The idea of leadership affirms the capacity of individuals to move, inspire, and mobilize masses of people so that they act together in pursuit of an end. Sometimes leadership serves good purposes, sometimes bad; but whether the end is benign or evil, great leaders are those men and women who leave their personal stamp on history.

Now, the very concept of leadership implies the proposition that individuals can make a difference. This proposition has never been universally accepted. From classical times to the present day, eminent thinkers have regarded individuals as no more than the agents and pawns of larger forces, whether the gods and goddesses of the ancient world or, in the modern era, race, class, nation, the dialectic, the will of the people, the spirit of the times, history itself. Against such forces, the individual dwindles into insignificance.

So contends the thesis of historical determinism. Tolstoy's great novel *War and Peace* offers a famous statement of the case. Why, Tolstoy asked, did millions of men in the Napoleonic wars, denying their human feelings and their common sense, move back and forth across Europe slaughtering their fellows? "The war," Tolstoy answered, "was bound to happen simply because it was bound to happen." All prior history predetermined it. As for leaders, they, Tolstoy said, "are but the labels that serve to give a name to an end and, like labels, they have the least possible connection with the event." The greater the leader, "the more conspicuous the inevitability and the predestination of every act he commits." The leader, said Tolstoy, is "the slave of history."

Determinism takes many forms. Marxism is the determinism of class. Nazism the determinism of race. But the idea of men and women as the slaves of history runs athwart the deepest human instincts. Rigid determinism abolishes the idea of human freedom—

the assumption of free choice that underlies every move we make, every word we speak, every thought we think. It abolishes the idea of human responsibility, since it is manifestly unfair to reward or punish people for actions that are by definition beyond their control. No one can live consistently by any deterministic creed. The Marxist states prove this themselves by their extreme susceptibility to the cult of leadership.

More than that, history refutes the idea that individuals make no difference. In December 1931 a British politician crossing Park Avenue in New York City between 76th and 77th Streets around 10:30 P.M. looked in the wrong direction and was knocked down by an automobile—a moment, he later recalled, of a man aghast, a world aglare: "I do not understand why I was not broken like an eggshell or squashed like a gooseberry." Fourteen months later an American politician, sitting in an open car in Miami, Florida, was fired on by an assassin; the man beside him was hit. Those who believe that individuals make no difference to history might well ponder whether the next two decades would have been the same had Mario Constasino's car killed Winston Churchill in 1931 and Giuseppe Zangara's bullet killed Franklin Roosevelt in 1933. Suppose, in addition, that Adolf Hitler had been killed in the street fighting during the Munich *Putsch* of 1923 and that Lenin had died of typhus during World War I. What would the 20th century be like now?

For better or for worse, individuals do make a difference. "The notion that a people can run itself and its affairs anonymously," wrote the philosopher William James, "is now well known to be the silliest of absurdities. Mankind does nothing save through initiatives on the part of inventors, great or small, and imitation by the rest of us—these are the sole factors in human progress. Individuals of genius show the way, and set the patterns, which common people then adopt and follow."

Leadership, James suggests, means leadership in thought as well as in action. In the long run, leaders in thought may well make the greater difference to the world. But, as Woodrow Wilson once said, "Those only are leaders of men, in the general eye, who lead in action. . . . It is at their hands that new thought gets its translation into the crude language of deeds." Leaders in thought often invent in solitude and obscurity, leaving to later generations the tasks of imitation. Leaders in action—the leaders portrayed in this series—have to be effective in their own time.

And they cannot be effective by themselves. They must act in response to the rhythms of their age. Their genius must be adapted, in a phrase of William James's, "to the receptivities of the moment." Leaders are useless without followers. "There goes the mob," said the French politician hearing a clamor in the streets. "I am their leader. I must follow them." Great leaders turn the inchoate emotions of the mob to purposes of their own. They seize on the opportunities of their time, the hopes, fears, frustrations, crises, potentialities. They succeed when events have prepared the way for them, when the community is awaiting to be aroused, when they can provide the clarifying and organizing ideas. Leadership ignites the circuit between the individual and the mass and thereby alters history.

It may alter history for better or for worse. Leaders have been responsible for the most extravagant follies and most monstrous crimes that have beset suffering humanity. They have also been vital in such gains as humanity has made in individual freedom, religious and racial tolerance, social justice and respect for human rights.

There is no sure way to tell in advance who is going to lead for good and who for evil. But a glance at the gallery of men and women in *World Leaders—Past and Present* suggests some useful tests.

One test is this: do leaders lead by force or by persuasion? By command or by consent? Through most of history leadership was exercised by the divine right of authority. The duty of followers was to defer and to obey. "Theirs not to reason why,/ Theirs but to do and die." On occasion, as with the so-called "enlightened despots" of the 18th century in Europe, absolutist leadership was animated by humane purposes. More often, absolutism nourished the passion for domination, land, gold and conquest and resulted in tyranny.

The great revolution of modern times has been the revolution of equality. The idea that all people should be equal in their legal condition has undermined the old structure of authority, hierarchy and deference. The revolution of equality has had two contrary effects on the nature of leadership. For equality, as Alexis de Tocqueville pointed out in his great study *Democracy in America*, might mean equality in servitude as well as equality in freedom.

"I know of only two methods of establishing equality in the political world," Tocqueville wrote. "Rights must be given to every citizen, or none at all to anyone . . . save one, who is the mast of all." There was no middle ground "between the sovereignty of and the absolute power of one man." In his astonishing prediction of 20th-century totalitarian dictatorship, Tocqueville explained how the revolution of equality could lead to the *"Führerprinzip"* and more terrible absolutism than the world had ever known.

But when rights are given to every citizen and the sovereignty of all is established, the problem of leadership takes a new form, becomes more exacting than ever before. It is easy to issue commands and enforce them by the rope and the stake, the concentration camp and the *gulag.* It is much harder to use argument and achievement to overcome opposition and win consent. The Founding Fathers of the United States understood the difficulty. They believed that history had given them the opportunity to decide, as Alexander Hamilton wrote in the first Federalist Paper, whether men are indeed capable of basing government on "reflection and choice, or whether they are forever destined to depend . . . on accident and force."

Government by reflection and choice called for a new style of leadership and a new quality of followership. It required leaders to be responsive to popular concerns, and it required followers to be active and informed participants in the process. Democracy does not eliminate emotion from politics; sometimes it fosters demagoguery; but it is confident that, as the greatest of democratic leaders put it, you cannot fool all of the people all of the time. It measures leadership by results and retires those who overreach or falter or fail.

It is true that in the long run despots are measured by results too. But they can postpone the day of judgment, sometimes indefinitely, and in the meantime they can do infinite harm. It is also true that democracy is no guarantee of virtue and intelligence in government, for the voice of the people is not necessarily the voice of God. But democracy, by assuring the right of opposition, offers built-in resistance to the evils inherent in absolutism. As the theologian Reinhold Niebuhr summed it up, "Man's capacity for justice makes democracy possible, but man's inclination to injustice makes democracy necessary."

A second test for leadership is the end for which power is sought. When leaders have as their goal the supremacy of a master race or the promotion of totalitarian revolution or the acquisition and exploitation of colonies or the protection of greed and privilege or the preservation of personal power, it is likely that their leadership will do little to advance the cause of humanity. When their goal is the abolition of slavery, the liberation of women, the enlargement of opportunity for the poor and powerless, the extension of equal rights to racial minorities, the defense of the freedoms of expression and opposition, it is likely that their leadership will increase the sum of human liberty and welfare.

Leaders have done great harm to the world. They have also conferred great benefits. You will find both sorts in this series. Even "good" leaders must be regarded with a certain wariness. Leaders are not demigods; they put on their trousers one leg after another just like ordinary mortals. No leader is infallible, and every leader needs to be reminded of this at regular intervals. Irreverence irritates leaders but is their salvation. Unquestioning submission corrupts leaders and demands followers. Making a cult of a leader is always a mistake. Fortunately hero worship generates its own antidote. "Every hero," said Emerson, "becomes a bore at last."

The signal benefit the great leaders confer is to embolden the rest of us to live according to our own best selves, to be active, insistent, and resolute in affirming our own sense of things. For great leaders attest to the reality of human freedom against the supposed inevitabilities of history. And they attest to the wisdom and power that may lie within the most unlikely of us, which is why Abraham Lincoln remains the supreme example of great leadership. A great leader, said Emerson, exhibits new possibilities to all humanity. "We feed on genius. . . . Great men exist that there may be greater men."

Great leaders, in short, justify themselves by emancipating and empowering their followers. So humanity struggles to master its destiny, remembering with Alexis de Tocqueville: "It is true that around every man a fatal circle is traced beyond which he cannot pass; but within the wide verge of that circle he is powerful and free; as it is with man, so with communities."

# 1
# High Priest of the Revolution

On a mild spring day in 1794, under a cloudless blue sky, one of the many startling spectacles of the French Revolution was about to unfold. That day, June 8, was the celebration of the Festival of the Supreme Being. About to lead the elaborate pageantry planned to begin in the Tuileries Gardens in Paris was a 36-year-old revolutionary, who was then the most influential member of the feared Committee of Public Safety. He was thin and diminutive in stature. His brow protruded above cold, penetrating eyes. Except for being meticulously well dressed, he appeared nondescript, almost drab. He had a habit of pushing his eyeglasses, then called preservers, onto his forehead, revealing an annoyed expression. The committee he headed, and the terror that was its chief weapon, became nearly synonymous with his name: Maximilien Robespierre.

While this carefully choreographed event spotlighted Robespierre at the pinnacle of power, it also placed him under the harsh scrutiny of his enemies. In seven weeks' time, he would perish by the guillotine, the instrument of death to which he had condemned so many others.

*The people will become easier to lead as the human mind acquires greater activity, light, force, and philosophy.*
—MAXIMILIEN ROBESPIERRE

**Maximilien Robespierre was briefly the most powerful man in his nation during the French Revolution. Like other revolutionary leaders, his downfall was brought about by the social and political turmoil he helped engineer.**

**The impulses for bloody revenge and democracy that characterized the French Revolution found perfect expression in the guillotine, the means of execution perfected in France during this period. Before 1792, only condemned aristocrats had the privilege of a swift and relatively painless decapitation.**

For the previous five years, France had experienced one abrupt and violent change after another. The revolution that had begun in Paris in 1789 was to become an unforgettable landmark in the history of the world. Heroes and villains were difficult to tell apart in the struggle to bring the French nation from under the shadow of absolute monarchy. This process was not accomplished in a day; there was no quick transition at bayonet point from tyranny to freedom. An entire society was sacrificed in the hope of bringing forth a new and better one. The mathematician and philosopher Marie-Jean-Antoine Caritat, marquis de Condorcet, explained that the revolution "was to embrace the entire economy of society, change every social relation, and find its way down to the furthest level of the political chain." About a month before the Festival of the Supreme Being, Condorcet died, some claim by his own hand, rather than face execution on the order of Robespierre's allies.

This drama took place on a panoramic stage, according to a convoluted script, with a multitude of players. A vast and intricate episode in Western history, it was also the first truly modern revolution. The most daring and noble precepts of the 18th century — those of democracy, equality, and individual freedom — were its driving forces. Not surprisingly, many forces collided during the long ordeal that shaped French government and society after the *ancien régime*, or old order, was destroyed. Every Frenchman seemed to pursue what he understood to be social justice. Yet oppressions and injustice swiftly took new forms during the resulting turmoil. In search of political freedom and equality, revolutionary France also produced some of the first models for modern dictatorships.

Probably few events in Western civilization have been as filled with paradox as the French Revolution. While essays defending human dignity flowed from the pens of French intellectuals and politicians, blood ran in the nation's streets. When the 19th-century English novelist Charles Dickens wrote of the French Revolution, "It was the best of times, it was the worst of times," he summed up the revolution's many puzzling contradictions.

In the moments before the pomp and festivities were to begin, Robespierre was living out the last days of his terrible power. As he was envisioning a nation built upon his all-consuming passion for virtue, Robespierre's adversaries were already plotting his downfall.

The National Convention, the revolution's ruling body, established in September 1792, had decided in October 1793 that "the government of France is revolutionary." This meant, in effect, that the government was the revolution. No one took this principle more seriously than Robespierre. Yet members of the Convention now suspected that the man about to lead this symbolic mass event was himself becoming too great a symbol. Robespierre's reputation had spread as far as England and Germany, countries in which he was increasingly regarded as the personification of the revolution.

The festival was also to serve as an inaugural ceremony. Four days earlier, Robespierre had suddenly

> *Morals are more powerful than laws, so it is incumbent upon us to uphold them, to improve them, so as to bring about the reign of virtue on earth, which produces happiness as the sun produces light.*
> —ROBESPIERRE

15

been swept to the heights of political authority. By a landslide vote, he had been elected president of the National Convention. Early the previous month, in a speech announcing the festival, he had boldly declared, "The French people recognize the being of a God and they recognize the immortality of the Soul," thus upholding the doctrines of the Deists. (Deism combined religious belief with reason, abandoning many other aspects of religious faith, but not God, whose existence it defended with rational arguments.) Robespierre and others felt that belief in a "supreme being" would help the revolution, not hinder it. A "Temple of Reason" would become the center for worship of this supreme being.

In a decree in May 1794, Robespierre declared that the citizens of the Republic were to hate tyrants, punish traitors, and defend justice and brotherhood. Through this cult, it seemed, Robespierre was determined to rid the Republic of all enemies. He attacked those who may have regarded new scientific discoveries, as well as the revolution's initial spirit of liberty, as reasons to reject belief in God, seizing the opportunity to reshape religious life in France. The new religion served Robespierre's unending revolution. There was apparently no end to the enemies of virtue, justice, and morality. The government and the people were never safe from conspirators. The Republic was the revolution, and the revolution in turn was a war against "the tyrant." For Robespierre, "the tyrant" was lurking everywhere. Tyranny and corruption had to be stamped out, no matter what guise these enemies might take. Certainly, Robespierre concluded, if good and evil existed (which to him they clearly did), there must also be a Supreme Being to reward the one and condemn the other.

Even though he had drifted away from the Roman Catholic church, the dominant faith in France, his rejection of atheism (the denial of God's existence) was final. In his May speech before the National Convention he had called atheism immoral and identified it with the aristocracy. Belief in the Supreme Being was necessary to a revolution based on reason, he insisted. Coincidentally, the festival took place on the Christian holiday of Whitsunday, although the Catholic faith had recently been banned.

A colorful procession, replete with banners and military music, began to make its way to the Champ de Mars, outside Paris. Atop an artificial mountain built for the occasion was placed a "Tree of Liberty." Near the tree stood a sculpture of two figures representing liberty and equality, symbolizing the French people. The march commenced with shouts of *Vive la République*. Voices rose, singing patriotic songs and a new hymn to the Supreme Being composed for the festival. Guns were fired in salute. Deputies to the Convention were dressed in new blue uniforms. At their waists were blue, white, and red sashes. Each deputy carried a sword. Plumes decorated their hats. The bouquets they carried added to the joyous colors that suffused the event. Houses and carriages were brightly decorated for the occasion. Bouquets of violets were carried by the children. Flowers were strewn everywhere.

A Parisian revolutionary delivers an impromptu call to arms in 1789, the year of the outbreak of the French Revolution. As the revolution progressed, those who continued to stir the people to action — and violence — became the nation's leaders.

ÉGALITÉ, LIBERTÉ.

COMITÉ DE SALUT PUBLIC

DE LA CONVÉNTION NATIONALE.,

Au nom de la République.

*A tous les Corps administratifs, & Officiers civils & militaires.*
*Laissez passer librement le Citoyen* Audetourfaend 20, Couriers
Charge d'eux députés pour les représentans près l'armée
De Aliit it prou le Neven natif de Fontainebleau Département
de Seine et marne âgé de 33 Ans taille de 5 pieds 6 pouces
cheveux et sourcils Bruns front couvert nez grand yeux
Gris bouche moyenne, menton rond, Visage
Ovale allant de Paret à l'armée du Rhin
à Strasbourg.

*Le présent Passe-port valable pour* le temps de sa Couste
*seulement*

*Fait au Comité de Salut Public, le* 22 Juin 1793, *l'an second*
*de la République Française.* Que et Invisible

Billaud Varenne    Carnot    Hérault    Robespierre

**Robespierre's signature appears on this passport issued by the Committee of Public Safety. The committee was the most powerful — and dangerous — arm of the revolutionary government.**

Before setting out on the march, Robespierre had paced nervously back and forth and said quietly, "I could say the whole world was here. . . . there are tyrants who will grow pale when they hear of this." He was certain that the absolute monarchs of Europe who took themselves for gods would quake at this public acknowledgment of the true god.

The festival was a strangely public display for such a secretive and rather unsociable man. In addition to the nearly 500,000 celebrants in Paris, people flocked to ceremonies throughout France that day. Robespierre was taking the first steps toward creating a new, official state religion. In his thinking, the revolution and the Republic could not be separated from the will of the Supreme Being. The Republic would be worshiped alongside the deity.

Amidst murmurings among the deputies, Robespierre led the throng to the site where five mannequinlike figures had been set up. Each effigy represented a vice that the revolution, according to Robespierre, would have to destroy. He was handed a torch, with which he ignited the figures representing atheism, ambition, egotism, discord, and false simplicity. Each effigy had been labeled "Sole Foreign Hope." This phrase referred to the peril posed by France's foreign enemies, who were united in opposing the revolution. As flames engulfed the figures Robespierre turned and said: "Let us rest only in our own constancy and our own virtue. Alone, but infallible guarantors of our own independence, let us crush the wicked league of kings even more by our greatness of character than by the force of our arms."

One final theatrical touch was to cap the event. The goddess of wisdom was to rise above the smoke and ashes left by the smoldering effigies. There were some onlookers who could not suppress hoots of laughter when the goddess appeared, for the mechanical deity was too damaged by smoke to be recognizable.

The new president of the Convention then began another speech. With only the slightest trace of excitement, Robespierre proclaimed: "God did not create kings to devour the human race. He did not create priests to harness us, like vile animals, to kings' chariots, and to give the world an example of baseness, pride, perfidy, debauchery, and lies; but he created men to help each other and to love each other and to arrive at happiness by the path of virtue." In the crowd, angry deputies turned to one another and whispered sarcastic comments about Robespierre's pompous words and actions. Here and there, even Parisian laborers and artisans, once his firmest supporters, seemed to express doubts. "Does he think he must also be God as well as the leader?" they grumbled.

While the ceremony gave reassurance to those who hoped that religious belief would be spared persecution in revolutionary France, other leaders wondered what Robespierre was up to. That same month they found out. Two days after the festival, the law of the 22nd Prairial was decreed. (France's revolutionary government had established a new calendar in 1792. The months were renamed, eliminating allusions to the past. The year 1792 was the Year One under the new calendar.) Under this law, all persons accused of political crimes were to be brought to Paris for judicial proceedings against them. The provincial courts were stripped of all authority in such cases. The law was formulated by Robespierre's most loyal and powerful lieutenants and was so strict that virtually any slip of the tongue could mean being charged with crimes against the state.

The law of the 22nd Prairial effectively stated that if the accused was found guilty, there was only one penalty: death. The Committee of Public Safety was made master of the National Convention and therefore of all France. With Robespierre as both president of the Convention and the most influential member of the Committee of Public Safety, anyone standing in the revolution's way could be executed. Robespierre's bloodthirsty colleague, the prosecutor Antoine-Quentin Fouquier-Tinville, could hardly wait to put the new law into operation. Referring to the dreaded guillotine, he said, "Next week, I'll be able to take the tops off three or four hundred." Some 1,220 people had already been sent to their deaths in this manner. Under the grisly policy known as the Reign of Terror, another 1,376 men, women, and even children were to be beheaded in the next seven weeks.

*The decree of that day — a decree drawn up in his own hand . . . may be stated in a single word, tyranny; but it was a tyranny such as never could last for a year on this earth, such as no remote lord of Africa could have exercised over his own bought slaves.*
—HILAIRE BELLOC
Robespierre biographer, on the law of the 22nd Prairial

Maximilien François Marie Isidore de Robespierre was born on May 6, 1758, four months after his parents were married in Arras, the humble capital of Artois province in northern France. His father, François Derobespierre, came from a family of lawyers. (Derobespierre was also Maximilien's surname until he began calling himself Robespierre around 1789.) The Derobespierres were an old and distinguished family whose members were solid and respected citizens of Arras. At least one ancestor's

An aristocrat is brought before the Revolutionary Tribune. During the Reign of Terror, instituted by Robespierre to preserve the revolution while France was at war, thousands of people were executed, based often on hearsay evidence or class resentment.

that of Blo-
rved in the
dy.

qualities
yhood at
a future
for him.
l, pass-
artner

Car-
ra                                    man.
Th                                    mid-
dle-                                  ick
suc                                   xi-
mili                                  st
child                            days of
life.

Max           never recovered from Jacque-

Rouget de l'Isle, composer of the "Marseillaise," sings the stirring song for the first time. His patriotic call to arms won popularity with prorevolution sympathizers and later became France's national anthem.

line's death. Never very stable, he quit practicing law, descended into deep depression, and drank heavily. When his eldest son was eight years old, he abandoned his family and tried to lose himself in travel. He reappeared intermittently in Arras until his death in Germany in 1777. Maximilien was entrusted to his maternal grandfather's care. His sisters, Charlotte and Henriette, were packed off to stay with their mother's sisters.

Clearly, his father's breakdown so soon after his mother's death had a telling impact on Maximilien's character, for from then on he seemed preoccupied with his future responsibility. While still a child, any

mention of his mother caused him to become sad and tears to come to his eyes.

Charlotte, the second eldest child, once remarked that her brother Maximilien "spoke to us with a kind of gravity which we respected." She, Maximilien, and their brother, Augustin Bon, were to remain close throughout the two brothers' lives. Augustin, not particularly successful at anything he tried, became one of his brother's most loyal camp followers during the revolution. Charlotte became engaged to the revolutionary Joseph Fouché, who eventually plotted against Robespierre. Charlotte later always firmly defended her brother, to whom

ENGLISH CHANNEL

Lille
Arras
ARTOIS
Le Havre
Rouen
Caen
ÎLE-DE-FRANCE
Reims
Évreux
Paris
Versailles
Seine
BRITTANY
NORMANDY
Rennes
Dijon
Nantes
VENDÉE
BURGUNDY
ALPS
Limoges
Lyon
BAY OF BISCAY
Grenoble
DAUPHINÉ
Bordeaux
Rhone
PROVENCE
Nîmes
Toulouse
Marseilles
PYRENEES
MEDITERRANEAN SEA

**Robespierre was born in the quiet northern city of Arras, France, in 1758. When he was 11 years old, he won a scholarship to a university in the nation's capital, Paris, the city that 20 years later would become the birthplace of the revolution.**

she remained devoted. Although Robespierre occasionally found her to be a nuisance because she involved herself in his private affairs, the two exchanged letters until his downfall.

Along with developing a strong sense of responsibility and seriousness, Robespierre also became humorless, unsmiling, and a loner — acquiring the outlook and demeanor that marked his later life. When it came to children's games, he preferred to enforce the rules rather than participate. Tending to withdraw from his schoolmates, he grew up silent, suspicious, and solitary. "He liked to be alone in order to think," Charlotte recorded simply.

From the outset, his education was provided by the Catholic church. As a child, he attended the Collège d'Arras. His teachers there were Oratorian priests, members of a religious order that emphasized public service. He learned the basics of Latin and public speaking. Years later, after his studies were completed, his relations with these priests remained favorable.

Robespierre was inclined to be a tattletale, reporting his schoolmates' misconduct — a trait that did not endear him to his fellows. Already demonstrating a capacity for concentration and hard work, the 11-year-old boy was awarded a scholarship by the abbey of Saint Vaast to the prestigious Collège de Louis-le-Grand, part of the University of Paris.

Usually a stern older brother, Robespierre gave all his toys to his sisters before journeying to Paris. On his way alone to the French capital, he knew his childhood was at an end.

# 2
# The Restless Reformer

At the Collège de Louis-le-Grand (named for King Louis XIV) Robespierre was educated with several other future revolutionaries. These included Louis-Marie Fréron and the flamboyant Camille Desmoulins. Both men later challenged Robespierre and his policies during the revolution. As youths, however, Desmoulins and Robespierre were on friendly terms. In contrast to many at the college, Desmoulins saw qualities worth admiring in the severe student from Arras. Nevertheless, years later, in 1794, Desmoulins was arrested and executed, one of the many victims of Robespierre's campaign to preserve the revolution.

Although the college was named for the 17th-century French ruler who had become the model for royal absolutism, the theory that kings derived their power from God had by now almost no adherents at the school. By the time Robespierre enrolled as a student in 1769, the college had undergone a significant change. The instructors were no longer priests of the Catholic church's Jesuit order. Those who were priests were Oratorians. The secular, or nonreligious, instructors, were eager to teach the new discoveries and ideas of the 18th century.

*We desire to substitute morality for egotism, probity for honor, duties for functions, the empire of reason for the tyranny of fashions.*
—ROBESPIERRE

---

**As he matured Robespierre's childhood idealism and self-discipline intensified. The liberal environment at Paris's Collège de Louis-le-Grand further developed his reformist tendencies.**

King Louis XIV, who ruled France from 1643 to 1715, promoted the idea that monarchs ruled by divine right. This theory was called into question during the Age of Reason, or Enlightenment, when a heightened interest in democracy and the theory that government should rule at the consent of the governed culminated in the French Revolution.

The Collège de Louis-le-Grand remained, however, under Catholic supervision. Its principal was a member of the clergy, but he tended to be lenient and did not interfere with the instructors' lessons. Discipline was not particularly strict. For serious students such as Robespierre, the atmosphere was conducive to a free exchange of information. He studied there for nine years.

Although the French Revolution was still 20 years away, an intellectual whirlwind had been stirred up in France. A revolution in French universities and in scholarly quarters was changing the way people thought about the universe, society, and the individual. Robespierre and his contemporaries were living in the Age of Reason, an era that would reach a climax in the French Revolution. Possibilities for change, progress, and individual freedom were all being explored with increasing boldness and curiosity. Robespierre immediately began to be exposed to these radical teachings.

One instructor on the faculty was the brilliant mathematician and philosopher Jean Le Rond d'Alembert. Along with other learned and innovative thinkers in France, d'Alembert contributed to the vast project that became the *Encyclopédie* (*Encyclopedia*). Those who wrote, compiled, and edited the *Encyclopédie* were known as the Encylopedists. Led by Denis Diderot, who served as editor-in-chief from 1751 until 1772, this project was the work of 18th-century France's most extraordinary thinkers and men of letters. Voltaire (the pseudonym of François Marie Arouet), the satirical genius and author of the famed novella *Candide*, was another famed contributer to the project.

Another celebrated contributor to the *Encyclopédie* was the social philosopher Jean-Jacques Rousseau, whose work had the most enduring and profound effect on Robespierre's political thinking. For Robespierre the most influential of Rousseau's works was the *Contrat Social* (*The Social Contract*), in which Rousseau argued that human beings are not naturally evil "but only corrupted and miserable." Before the rise of civilization and governments, man lived free and uncorrupted, according to Rousseau. Studying this work persuaded Robespierre that society had degraded and enslaved mankind. "Force," wrote Rousseau, "made the first slaves, and slavery, by degrading and corrupting its victims, perpetuated their bondage." The young Robespierre was also deeply impressed by Rousseau's claim that the state, or "sovereign," was the people themselves, and that they, in turn, were "master of all their goods." Contrary to popular claims, Rousseau did not believe that reason alone was the key to human progress. In *The Social Contract*, Rousseau systematically explained how to construct a society based upon what he called the "general will." The general will "is always right and tends always to the public advantage," Rousseau asserted.

Condorcet remarked that the learned *philosophes* were more concerned with spreading the truth than with actually discovering it. The Encyclopedists did indeed wish to bring the principles of reason and

Denis Diderot, the chief editor of the *Encyclopédie*, was one of the great figures of the Enlightenment, which was characterized by a belief in reason as the driving force behind social, political, scientific, and intellectual progress. He wrote novels, essays, and plays that attacked traditions he considered outmoded.

progress to as many people as they could. In this way, they were expanding the influence of the movement known as the Enlightenment. That such ideas presented a danger to the existing public order is illustrated by the close scrutiny the work received from government censors.

The political philosopher Charles-Louis de Secondat, baron de Montesquieu, was another noted contributor. His best-known works were *Les Lettres persanes* (*The Persian Letters*) and *L'Esprit des Lois* (*The Spirit of the Laws*). The latter was a major influence on the leaders of the American Revolution, which took place from 1775 to 1783, and on the French Revolution. In this work, Montesquieu set out to show that laws made by governments (and governments themselves) resulted from "the nature of things." He tried to study society scientifically and show that nature and the actual physical environment largely determined a people's form of government. Diderot's Encyclopedists borrowed extensively from Montesquieu's writings.

Progressive political and economic thought became more important as the Industrial Revolution began to transform the old economies of Europe, particularly in France and England. While factories and mills became more numerous, so did the educated and professional middle classes. Unlike the aristocracy, these classes did not inherit their wealth; they earned it through manufacturing and providing professional services. In France, they grew restless as their economic power grew. The nobles and aristocrats, who inherited from their feudal ancestors the right to rule over the land they owned, appeared to have their own government, whereas the middle classes still had no say concerning how France was governed. Although both the middle classes, or *bourgeoisie*, and aristocracy invested in land, the aristocrats still controlled most of the wealth in France. Buoyed by their growing economic strength, these newly developing classes pressured the ancien régime for changes.

During the 1700s, it was commonly felt that the human reason championed by the Encyclopedists would not only unlock the secrets of nature and

*What is good and conformable to order, is so from the nature of things, and independently of human conventions. All justice flows from God, and if we knew how to receive it from on high, we should require neither government nor laws.*

—JEAN-JACQUES ROUSSEAU
French philosopher
from *The Social Contract*

experience, but also serve as a beacon lighting a path to a perfect government, and ultimately a perfect society, or utopia. Robespierre's schoolmasters absorbed the teachings of the Encyclopedists and made them an extremely important part of what the students learned.

Also widely popular among Robespierre's teachers was the concept of republican government. The notion of a state not ruled by an absolute monarch, and that included limited participation by the common people, was appealing to the middle classes and some aristocrats. Deriving from the Latin words *res publica* (public matter), the first republic was founded in ancient Rome in 509 B.C. Robespierre was taught about the great statesmen of the Roman Republic. Most revered as enduring examples of good leadership were Tiberius and Gaius Gracchus (both noted reformers), as well as Brutus and Cicero. A 1st-century B.C. orator and philosopher, Cicero had a profound influence on the leaders of the

Many educated Frenchmen looked to the Roman Republic as a model of enlightened government. The 1st-century B.C. orator, statesman, and philosopher Marcus Tullius Cicero exemplified the democratic ideals of ancient Rome to many French revolutionaries.

General George Washington (on white horse) leads his troops against the British. The success of the American Revolution, which was seen as a victory for democratic principles, helped inspire popular unrest in France.

American Revolution and the democratic government it produced. Brutus had slain Julius Caesar, whom the Romans feared had sought to establish a hereditary monarchy. James Madison, U.S. president and one of the authors of the U.S. Constitution, popularized the term *republic* in the United States as meaning a representative government rather than a participatory democracy, a distinction made earlier by Montesquieu. These Roman statesmen were thought not only to stand for republican principles but also to be pillars of virtue. It was probably this conclusion that caused Robespierre to look upon civic virtue and the public trust as essential. Compared with the Roman Republic of antiquity, the French monarchy seemed hardly satisfactory.

Robespierre never displayed academic abilities much out of the ordinary. Yet through dedication and hard work he became in 1775 the college's prize student in Latin, an accomplishment that earned him the honor of greeting King Louis XVI and Queen Marie Antoinette. Eighteen years later, as a leading deputy to the future National Convention, Robespierre would vote to behead the king.

For this encounter with royalty Robespierre did what he could with his meager funds to obtain an acceptable suit of clothes and new shoes. The king was to pass by and review the Collège de Louis-le-Grand. Robespierre, the future revolutionary and scourge of the revolution's enemies, was asked to declaim a speech to the king in Latin.

Fatigued from his journey to Paris from Rheims, Louis remained in his carriage that day in July 1775 and paid scant attention to the pale student who stood reading aloud as a steady rain began to fall. Soon the king's carriage drove on. As the rain soaked his new shoes and clothes, Robespierre finished reading his Latin master's praises of the new king. The king was only four years older than the unknown student. The English writer Hilaire Belloc states that after the strange drama, "a rare and momentary light was to put these two in view for ever." In 1780 Robespierre earned his law degree from the University of Paris. He won a prize of 600 *livres* "for good conduct" as well as a scholarship. Generously, he persuaded the authorities to award the prize money to his brother, Augustin Bon. A year later, Robespierre was admitted to practice in Paris before France's most important court, but after failing to secure a valued and much needed patronage, he returned to provincial Arras. He began his career as a barrister with the Superior Council of Artois in November 1781. He was helped in getting started in his practice by a respected lawyer, Maître Liborel. Accustomed to living modestly, Robespierre took on cases that allowed him to display his high regard for social virtue and justice. (His future political opponent, the revolutionary Georges Jacques Danton, in contrast, took any case, regardless of the principle involved.) This helped Robespierre's reputation immensely, and he soon commanded the admiration of many in Arras. In 1782 Robespierre argued slightly more than a dozen cases. Usually encouraging clients to settle out of court, he also seemed to care little about the amount of his fee.

That same year, the Oratorians, who remembered their pupil Robespierre from his days at the Collège

*[The effect of a republic is] to refine and enlarge the public views, by passing them through the medium of a chosen body of citizens, whose wisdom may best discern the true interest of their country, and whose patriotism and love of justice will be least likely to sacrifice it to temporary or partial considerations.*
—JAMES MADISON
American politician,
from *The Federalist Papers*

In *The Social Contract*, 18th-century philosopher and author Jean-Jacques Rousseau wrote that "man is born free, and everywhere he is in chains." The young Robespierre was fascinated by Rousseau's ideas.

d'Arras, called on him to speak at an award presentation. He complied and gave a speech in honor of King Henry IV, who had reconstructed the French nation after its economy was shattered by foreign and civil wars during the 16th century. While attending to this engagement, Robespierre became aware of how many fellow lawyers and judges were concerned with the increasing need for reforms in France.

Appointed a judge, or magistrate, in March 1782, Robespierre came into increased contact with prominent citizens. Many of them thought that Louis XVI would have the vision and wisdom that Henry IV had demonstrated. Robespierre agreed. In the early 1780s he saw no "remedy for a specific ill" in overthrowing the king. Instead, he believed that gradual, step-by-step reform would solve France's many difficulties. At this time an opponent of capital punishment, he once spent two sleepless nights struggling with his responsibility as a magistrate to impose the death penalty on a convicted murderer.

After Robespierre was forced to give up his association with Liborel, he became a protégé of Maître Buissart. Buissart subsequently became a trusted friend and political ally during the next few years. One case Robespierre tried brought him considerable notoriety as a barrister. Involving a retired barrister named de Vissery, the case touched upon "the cause of science and the arts," as Buissart put it. Enlightenment reason was jousting with superstition and ignorance. At issue were fears of an unfamiliar invention — the lightning rod, or conductor — and an individual's right to attach such a device to his own house. The townspeople complained to the authorities, thinking the invention an offense against the heavens. No amount of explanation about electricity could dissuade the bailiff from ordering the lightning rod's removal.

Experiments of a similar nature had been conducted by French scientists as early as 1752. The American statesman, amateur scientist, and envoy to France, Benjamin Franklin, had demonstrated that lightning and electricity were the same phenomenon. Thinking the bailiff's action unjustified, de Vissery filed an appeal with the Council of Artois. No scientist himself, Robespierre argued the brief written, for the most part, by Buissart. His speeches were eloquent, and he managed to portray the sciences as being on the side of heaven. He likened his client to such celebrated scientists as Galileo and the medical pioneer William Harvey (whose work revealed the nature of the body's circulatory system). Robespierre tried to show that the lightning rod was an effective defense against lightning's destructive power. The favorable verdict he received was a public victory for the ideals of the Encyclopedists and the Enlightenment.

Robespierre was well aware of the publicity to be gained from the decision. De Vissery was obliged to pay for printing his lawyer's arguments. Ready to use these materials to his benefit, Robespierre then sent the printed editions to fellow jurists and barristers. Even the very famous (none of whom he knew personally) received copies. One such figure

*Within a few months the [Magistrate's] duties disgusted a character in which the demand for reform and the faith in Rousseau were yet profoundly sincere.*
—HILAIRE BELLOC
Robespierre biographer

was Benjamin Franklin himself. Buissart, meanwhile, published his pleadings from the case in the newspaper *Le Mercure de France*. Seeing fit to commend Robespierre, Buissart mentioned the young lawyer's contributions in the newspaper.

While living in Arras, Robespierre became active as a writer on political and legal issues of the day. His interest in writing and in current events began to overshadow his interest in practicing law. He composed several essays, some of which won prizes. His essays during this period concentrated on moral issues. One prize-winning piece, written for a contest sponsored by the Academy of Metz in 1784, dealt with the increasing interest in what society should do with its criminals and the mentally ill. Robespierre's essay discussed the stigma cast upon families with members involved in criminal activity and, reflecting the view most frequently held by the intellectuals of the day, took a position against holding the family responsible for one of its members' actions. So, of course, did the other contestants, but it was Robespierre who won the second place award, which amounted to 400 livres. In this essay he showed a flair for a controlled, usually polite style. As was then customary, he couched his ideas in language that praised the king for the good he was expected to perform.

Literary and scientific clubs were springing up in France wherever there were enough middle-class intellectuals and professionals to support them. Robespierre was a member of just such a group, the Academy of Arras, which he joined in 1783. It was during this time that he rented a house for himself and his sister Charlotte. Without much success, Charlotte and his aunts played matchmakers to the ambitious bachelor. He also joined a literary club. The club brought together an odd assortment of provincial gentlemen. They called themselves the Rosati. The group's members consisted of a painter, the vicar of St. Aubert, two priests, a surgeon, and several musicians. Joseph Fouché, who had studied with the Oratorians, although without ever taking the vows of the priesthood, first met Robespierre through this group. The young lawyer took a liking

Camille Desmoulins delivers a speech during the early days of the revolution. Although Robespierre and Desmoulins were friends during their youth, Robespierre had his old schoolmate executed in 1794 after he opposed Robespierre's repressive government.

to Fouché almost at once. With her brother's full approval, Charlotte and Fouché soon became romantically interested in each other.

These were happy times for Robespierre — possibly the only period in his life when he was gregarious and lively. On his days off, he picnicked, danced, and sang. The young women he met during outings, literary readings, and musical performances found him charming. Nevertheless, it seems he had his eye on his public career rather than romance. Charlotte insisted that her brother and the stepdaughter of one of his aunts were then very much in love. His sister also claimed that he was heartbroken when he discovered that the young woman had decided to marry another man. It is quite likely that Robespierre had never proposed to her.

During this period Robespierre followed a strict regimen. There were few free moments. He got up at 6:00 A.M. and worked in his study until 8:00 A.M. After breakfast he walked to the courthouse buildings to begin the day's business. His evenings were equally busy and clocklike in their organization. Robespierre also was preoccupied with his appearance. He took pains to dress with extreme neatness and often looked at himself in the mirror. Each morning a barber shaved him and powdered his wig. This meticulous regard for his appearance remained with him to his death.

By June 1786 Robespierre was presiding over the Academy of Arras as director. Under his leadership, the academy did not exclude women as members. One woman whom he publicly honored in a speech was Mademoiselle Keralio, the author of several novels. Keralio was the daughter of an obscure historian. She herself aspired to write a comprehensive world history, starting with the ancient past. She moved to Paris when the revolution broke out and coedited a newspaper, *Le Mercure National*, with her husband, a radical journalist. In the revolution's early days, she was outspoken in her support of Robespierre.

As for his law practice, Robespierre soon enough found himself in contests that tested his mettle but offered little monetary reward. Disinterested in financial gain, he preferred cases that offered him the limelight and even some sensationalism. In 1786 he became embroiled in a case involving a poor ropemaker, François Deteuf, who was accused of robbing the nearby abbey of Anchin, where Benedictine monks were housed. The ropemaker hired Robespierre to defend him. The monk who lodged the complaint against the unsuspecting ropemaker was seized and placed under arrest on information given by the church authorities. It seemed that this monk, as keeper of the abbey's treasury, had pilfered the funds and used them for his own purposes.

The charge against Deteuf was dropped. Deteuf was the earliest example of Robespierre championing the interests of the working class in order to further his own goals. In the Deteuf case it was notoriety Robespierre sought, whereas in later years he would gain political power through the support of the workers and artisans. The impoverished rope-maker was the perfect client for Robespierre, a lawyer with a social conscience who was also determined to create a controversial reputation for himself. Deteuf, his counselor said, had suffered great damage to his own honor and reputation and deserved compensation. By this time the monk who had been convicted for the theft was languishing in prison. Robespierre turned on the monk's superiors and accused them of knowing all along of their treasurer's wrongdoing and immoral conduct. The Benedictine abbey, Robespierre claimed, should pay his client 30,000 livres in damages. Before the trial was concluded, Robespierre published what were considered outrageous remarks. His arguments attacked both the monks, who already had brought to justice one of their own, and the magistrates who ruled in the case. They were miscarrying justice, he said. He high-handedly accused the court of actually encouraging wrongdoing and terrorizing an innocent defendant. The magistrates were offended. The Benedictine monks were appalled. Liborel, Robespierre's former mentor, was convinced that the arrogant barrister had gone too far and published a denunciation of Robespierre's ruthless tactics in which he stated that Robespierre should be punished for his "infamous libel."

The young lawyer had stirred up a hornets' nest. The revolutionary within him had lashed out against the clergy and the courts, two established forces of the old order. Arras hummed with debate. The clergy was sharply divided over Robespierre and Deteuf. Arrayed against him were the abbey of Anchin, of course, whose monks were not at all reform-minded, and the Council of Artois. His defenders were his old friends the Oratorian priests, the bishop, and the barristers. Eventually, the rope-maker agreed to accept 6,000 livres to settle the case and call off his troublesome lawyer. Although his client dismissed him and paid him a relatively small fee, Robespierre had succeeded in making the case into a crusade.

Louis XVI takes the coronation oath at Rheims Cathedral in 1775. Following the ceremony, Louis had his first meeting with Robespierre, but the new king paid little attention to the earnest young student who would become one of France's most ruthless revolutionaries.

In another case, in 1787, Robespierre's arguments became increasingly vehement and politically inspired. Again he charged the magistrates of Arras with using the law to crush the poor and disenfranchised. "Do you know why there are so many needy?" he wrote. Answering his own question, he charged the judiciary with clutching society's wealth in its own "greedy hands."

In still another case Robespierre once again showed that broader political problems were his real concern. The case concerned a deserter from the military who was unjustly imprisoned in a mental asylum. Robespierre began by condemning the king's *lettres de cachet*. These letters contained secret orders from the king that allowed people to be imprisoned without a formal charge or any trial. He used the prisoner's case as another issue on which to base his oratory and pamphleteering. He de-

nounced the monks who looked after the prisoner. Once again, he printed his pleadings and arguments, which attacked the legal system that prevailed under the monarchy. This time he sent a copy to one of the king's most renowned advisers, Jacques Necker, whom Robespierre would meet in Versailles the next year. In a covering letter, he praised this figure as a great citizen capable of leading an "interesting revolution."

As Robespierre's reputation grew, his law practice dwindled, and his finances suffered. Fellow barristers no longer referred cases to him. Writing did not produce the results he wanted. In 1788 he was at any rate determined to train his sights on the rough and tumble of politics. While the king's reputation for stubbornness and bumbling grew, tensions between the privileged classes and the underclasses were reaching an all-time high.

# 3

# Kingdom in Crisis

Louis XVI possessed few of the qualities of the earlier Bourbon kings. (The Bourbons were descendants of Henry IV, who died in 1610.) Louis's flaws as a leader made him most closely resemble his grandfather, Louis XV, who reigned from 1715 until 1774 and was particularly unsteady at the helm. Since the king lacked the ability and character to lead his cabinet ministers, they tended to pursue their own individual policies, which often conflicted with one another.

During the reign of Louis XIV, known as the Sun King, the bishop and theologian Jacques-Bénigne Bossuet propounded the arguments for absolute monarchy and the divine right of kings. Prior to the Sun King's reign, which lasted from 1643 to 1715, it was thought that the church and the king should be kept separate and independent. Bossuet declared that the king represented God's will on earth. He wrote, "This is the image of God who seated on his throne in the highest heaven sets the whole of nature in motion." For his part, Louis XIV had little doubt that his power was absolute. "L'état c'est moi" ("I am the state"), he is reputed to have said.

*Never was any such event so inevitable yet so completely unforeseen.*
—ALEXIS DE TOCQUEVILLE
on the French Revolution

**Robespierre wears the powdered wig and ponytail that were popular among the upper classes in Europe and America during the 18th century. Despite his upper-middle-class birth, Robespierre became a champion of the poor and powerless.**

Louis XVI inherited financial problems as well as the crown and a legacy of absolutism. His predecessors, Louis XIV and Louis XV, squandered the royal treasury on a succession of wars. Under the Sun King, famine and persecution of the Huguenots (French Protestants) also put a strain on the economy, whereas a financial panic in the early years of the reign of Louis XV caused further economic problems.

To solve these problems, the French kings resorted to a traditional measure — taxes. By 1749 a tax called the *vingtième* was instituted. It was intended to apply to all landholders, regardless of social status, but corruption soon prevented the tax from being collected. Both the middle and noble classes concealed their incomes, and the peasants were ultimately forced to pay this tax as well as a traditional land tax, the *taille*, and other taxes.

The economic troubles worsened after the Seven Years' War, which lasted from 1756 to 1763, and dissenting voices began to make themselves heard, mainly from the nobility, who claimed that their privileges were being threatened by the crown. France was forced to default on many of its debts.

**Thousands of Huguenots (French Protestants) were massacred by Catholics on St. Bartholomew's Eve, 1572. France's long history of religious warfare, which damaged the economy and divided the population, had repercussions that lasted through the period of the revolution.**

By 1788 bankruptcy began gradually gnawing at the treasury. In addition, many aristocrats were living on notes and lines of credit. To add to this growing difficulty, income from wine production, an important industry in France, seriously declined. As revenues trickled away, the government continued to pursue fruitless policies, subsidizing the unprofitable New India Company, dedicated to trade with the East Indies, and buoying up the Paris Water Company — which supplied no water. The government, meanwhile, ignored the plight of the poor, whose problems became a potential threat as their numbers increased.

Louis XVI was far from godlike. Indecisive by nature, he lacked virtually every quality necessary to be a successful ruler. He was spoiled and childish, a practical joker with a dull mind and slovenly habits. Ill-equipped to deal with matters of state, he let his cabinet ministers struggle with the emergencies that faced his kingdom. Although he possessed tremendous energy, he devoted most of it to outings, hunting, and tinkering in his workshop. He enjoyed making objects out of brass. Statecraft was not one of his skills.

By the late 18th century, about 92 percent of France's 26 million people supported themselves through agriculture. As the king's government became increasingly oppressive during the late 1700s, the taille drained the small incomes of peasant farmers, who comprised the majority of the population.

The nobility, who made up a very small percentage of the population, owned a disproportionately large percentage of the land. In Montpelier, for example, the nobility accounted for only 3 percent of those who owned property but they held 20 percent of the land. Such landowners were also exempt from paying the oppressive taille.

France's ill-clad, malnourished peasantry reminded the visiting Scottish novelist Tobias Smollett of "ravenous scarecrows." Being at the bottom of an oppressive hierarchy, they carried French society's heaviest burdens. While the noble *seigneurs* (lords) who controlled France's feudal manors were

*Many noblemen in fact were far less well off than the increasingly prosperous urban middle classes whom they considered quite as great a threat to their privileged existence as royal absolutism.*
—CHRISTOPHER HIBBERT
British historian

It was hoped that Louis XVI would act decisively to end France's social injustices and economic woes, but he proved to be an ineffective leader who watched as his nation's problems mounted.

still taking both land and bread from the farmers, two emerging classes were having an impact on French society. These were the urban working class and the urban poor, or *sans-culottes* — "those without breeches" — and the middle classes, or bourgeoisie. Members of the middle classes included men like Robespierre. They were lawyers, magistrates, and businessmen. Some had even bought manors, tracts of land, and estates, which they ran as seigneurs. More than any other class or group, they were frustrated by the king's desire to protect the stagnant social system, which exploited the poor and withheld basic freedoms and rights for everyone. The aristocrats felt that it was only just to take some power away from the crown. They wanted to put an end to the king's absolute rule, which enabled him to govern without constitutional restrictions. Meanwhile, the growing middle classes envied the aristocracy's privileges and inherited wealth. The bourgeoisie had targeted the nobility as their chief enemy and were determined to get at them — even if it meant endangering the social hierarchy by cooperating with the lower classes.

The French monarchy did not permit any legislative body to take part in governing the country — or even to exist, for that matter. There were, however, 13 institutions called *parlements*. The parlements were actually courts of appeal. Their responsibility was to register the king's edicts, or official orders, as well as various tax-related laws. Magistrates who sat on these courts came exclusively from the noble classes. Most prominent were the parlements of Bordeaux, Grenoble, Metz, Rouen, Toulouse, and Paris.

The Paris Parlement was the most venerable of them all because a large proportion of its members were from the *ancienne race*, meaning that their noble titles dated from the 15th and 16th centuries. This parlement's decisions affected as many as 10 million people. By the 18th century the parlements were firmly under the control of the king and were occasionally punished when they challenged royal authority. In fact, the entire Paris Parlement was sent into exile in 1720. In 1771 the Paris Parlement was forcibly disbanded after it led a rebellion. Longing for the power to veto the king's commands, the parlements sometimes exploited their popularity with the common people for selfish ends. Although the Paris Parlement was a potential representative branch of government, it acted only for the interests of the nobility.

In early 1787, Charles-Alexandre Calonne, the king's director-general of finance, urged the Assembly of Notables, a convention of nobles, prominent officials, priests, and magistrates, to accept substantial financial reforms in order to salvage the teetering economy and avoid widespread unrest. The notables angrily objected. The taxes he had in mind would ruin France. It was not for them to suffer, they insisted, in order to make the kingdom solvent.

Calonne's attempt at practicality was not politically wise. Previous finance ministers had also been unable to force the upper classes to face the reality of the economic crisis. Rather than risk the wrath of the nobility and clergy by insisting on reform, they borrowed money or used other strategies. The

> *[A]lthough* parlement *was far more concerned with its interests than with those of the nation at large, it had come to be regarded, in the people's mind, as their champion.*
> —CHRISTOPHER HIBBERT
> British historian

Swiss banking millionaire Jacques Necker, who first served as finance minister from 1776 to 1781, simply declared that there was a surplus in the government treasury, which only increased the wrath of the notables when Calonne told them changes had to be made. Necker's successors were forced to resign when they were unable to devise painless ways to cure the economy. The notables were joined in their anger at Calonne by Queen Marie Antoinette, who took exception to his statements on the role corruption had played in the instability of the economy. Calonne was forced into exile and replaced by Loménie de Brienne, the archbishop of Toulouse.

**Her child clutching at her skirts, a Frenchwoman pleads with unsympathetic officials in this engraving entitled "Victims of History." France's middle and lower classes staggered under a heavy burden of taxation during the years prior to the revolution.**

After Brienne announced in July 1788 that a meeting of the Estates-General was scheduled for May 1789 in Versailles, the king called for a meeting of the parlements. The Paris Parlement became agitated by Brienne's insistence on new stamp and land taxes, which had also been called for by Calonne. The parlement claimed that the only body or assembly that could legally vote for such taxes was the Estates-General, a medieval lawmaking body that had not been convoked since Louis XIII was king, 175 years earlier.

In retaliation, Brienne ordered the Paris Parlement to withdraw to Troyes in July 1787. By May 1788 the parlement had been told that its judicial powers were revoked. This action stirred the parlements to rebel. It was a turning point for the nobility. Their violent reaction to this attack on their power and privileges led to a revolt sometimes referred to as the *révolte nobilaire*. There were uprisings in towns where the parlements were based.

In August 1788 Louis himself announced that the Estates-General would be convoked in May 1789. The Paris Parlement asked that this assembly be made up of equal numbers of representatives from each estate, or order of society. In this way the Third Estate (those who were not clergy or nobles) would be guaranteed to lose in any vote against the other two estates. (The First Estate was the clergy, the Second the nobility.) Brienne, meanwhile, resigned shortly after finding that Calonne's judgments regarding France's economy had been accurate.

Although the First Estate and the Second Estate had definite disagreements, they both represented the forces of privilege. There was little doubt that a built-in voting advantage in the Estates-General would encourage the First and Second Estates to band together to protect their privileged political status. The Third Estate's hopes for easing the tax burden on the people would be dashed. However, the members of the Second Estate had also grown uneasy with the absolutism of the monarchy. They regarded their own powers and privileges as among the few institutions in France capable of checking the king's power.

> *What is the third estate? Everything. What has it been up till now in the political order? Nothing. What does it desire to be? Something.*
> —EMMANUEL JOSEPH SIEYÈS
> French political activist

This drawing from 1789 shows figures representing France's privileged classes, the landed nobility and clergy, who controlled most of the nation's wealth, astride an emaciated figure symbolizing the nation's downtrodden lower classes.

Louis was urged to bring Necker back as director-general of finance, which he did with reluctance. In November 1788 Necker emphatically argued before the Assembly of Notables that the proposed system for the Estates-General would not do. In this regard Necker agreed with certain views of the Abbé Emmanuel-Joseph Sieyès, who produced an influential pamphlet in 1789 entitled "What Is the Third Estate?" The abbé's short piece also served to popularize the later widely held opinion that the privileged orders were parasites who survived on the labor of the poor. Sieyès also suggested that the Estates-General be free to conduct its business without interference.

Necker came to support the idea of "double representation," which meant that the Third Estate would have as many members as the other two combined. After much argument he obtained the king's approval of this plan. When the Estates-General met in 1789, the clergy had 300 members, the nobility 291 members, and the commons, 610 members.

Meanwhile, Robespierre was dissatisfied and frustrated with the progress of his career. When the news of the calling of the Estates-General reached Artois province in August 1788, he got to work. He wrote an 80-page pamphlet entitled "An Appeal to the Artesian People," in which he listed and explained the typical complaints heard in the region. It quickly became something of a bestseller in Artois. Robespierre's pamphlet was intended to stir up public opinion and served to announce that he was throwing his hat into the political ring. He followed this essay with several more. In March 1789 he formally announced his candidacy as a deputy to the Estates General. He closed his statement with a reference to the Supreme Being, expressing the hope that the Supreme Being would hear and answer his prayers. During this period he began to claim for himself the incorruptibility for which he later became famous. He was untarnished and would remain so, he insisted.

**Three members of the Estates-General are featured in this drawing. At left is a member of the Second Estate, or nobility; at the far right is a member of the First Estate, or clergy. At center is a member of the Third Estate or commons, which represented the middle class.**

NOBLESSE.

TIERS-ETAT.

CLERGY.

Politician and orator Honoré-Gabriel Riqueti, comte de Mirabeau, was a nobleman who championed the interests of the middle classes in the Estates-General and National Assembly. Although he was an early leader of the revolution, his moderate stands and ties with the monarchy eventually lessened his popularity.

His brother Augustin demonstrated his loyalty by campaigning for Robespierre throughout the province. Although some funding was necessary, Robespierre's campaign costs were not very great. For help with these expenses he looked to his old friend Maître Buissart. Buissart and his wife were well connected. They knew members of both the wealthy middle classes and the nobility in the area who were willing to contribute to the outspoken young barrister's campaign. The election process established for the Estates-General was so complex that it took five months before its members were finally selected. Ballots were distributed in December 1788. In January 1789 elections were officially decreed for the Third Estate, or commons.

Actual voting finally started on March 23, 1789. Deputies were indirectly elected. Delegates were appointed to an electoral assembly, which then chose the deputies. Delegates were chosen by a group called a corporation. Robespierre's radical beliefs were in evidence even before he was actually elected. He was soon at odds with the electoral process itself. When the mayor of Arras tried to take over the process, Robespierre supported another lawyer's demand that a commission be appointed rather than allow one man to tabulate the electors' votes. He apparently took his colleague's position as his own and argued that the people should not be cheated of their "sovereign rights" to be represented by those whom they in fact elected. Robespierre and a lawyer known as Maître Demazières attacked those who stood in the way of a fair electoral process, charging that those who opposed their view were the puppets of "despotism." On April 26 Robespierre was one of eight chosen to represent the commons of Arras.

Before setting out for Versailles, where the Estates-General was to convene, the newly elected deputies from Artois met together in a cathedral in Arras on May 1. Two days later all the deputies converged on Versailles, the site of Louis XIV's vast palace. On the three roads to the palace were crowds of merrymakers and curiosity seekers. Having left his modest fame behind him in Arras, Robespierre did not stand out.

On this fateful journey, Robespierre made certain to bring with him several copies of his essay "An Appeal to the Artesian People." The events in which he was about to take part were largely due to the protests written by leading political essayists from around France. One such essayist, the flamboyant and controversial Honoré-Gabriel Riqueti, comte de Mirabeau, would emerge as a significant leader in the Estates-General and the National Assembly, which succeeded it. Exiled at his father's request in 1775 and later imprisoned from 1777 until 1782, Mirabeau attacked the king's legal powers as unconstitutional in his famed work *Lettres de Cachet*, written while in prison. To the many rousing and brilliant pamphlets that circulated in 1788 Mirabeau added his "Appeal to the Provençal Nation."

The day following the deputies' arrival in Versailles, a celebration was held in the nearby cathe-

Louis's liberal finance minister Jacques Necker is carried on the shoulders of the marquis de Lafayette and the duke of Orléans (both members of the nobility who sympathized with France's lower classes) in this contemporary cartoon entitled "The Constitution of France."

The Estates-General convened for the first time in 175 years on May 5, 1789. Many historians consider this historic meeting as the start of the French Revolution.

dral to honor France's first national assembly since 1614. After finding a hotel, where he stayed with a group of deputies, Robespierre sought out Necker.

Over dinner the royal official graciously met with the earnest provincial deputy. Robespierre was soon in disagreement with Necker, who tried to recruit the deputy to his own thinking. Robespierre had hoped that Necker would take a more radical stance. The two men were worlds apart and could not be reconciled. Disappointed almost at once, Robespierre began to evaluate the more prominent dep-

uties, noting their deficiencies. Mirabeau, for example, had a reputation for scandal and recklessness. Robespierre could tolerate neither, even in a statesman as skilled as Mirabeau. Although Mirabeau was a noble, he was shunned by his own class. By becoming a deputy from Aix-en-Provence, he had tried to prove himself to the haughty nobles who rejected him. To Robespierre, the revolution went well beyond the selfish desires of individuals.

# 4

# The Deputy

In the rue des Chantiers, in one of the buildings set aside for the Estates-General, the clergy, the nobility, and the commons were ready to conduct the business at hand. At the head of the room sat the king. To his right were seated the deputies representing the clergy; to his left were those repesenting the nobility. At the rear of the room, facing the king, were the deputies from the commons. Among them was Maximilien Robespierre.

What was the Third Estate? asked its defender, Sieyès, in his pamphlet. It was nothing, but it aspired to be *something*, he wrote. The English historian Christopher Hibbert writes that in the Third Estate there were "some [who] believed that their ends should be obtained by agreement with the king and others [who] insisted that there must be no compromise even at the risk of violence." Robespierre did not seem to support violent measures just yet. As for the First Estate, certain priests, such as Sieyès and the radical Abbé Henri Grégoire, advocated change. There were others, such as Abbé Jean-Siffrein Maury and the older bishops, who defended the current system. Among the Second Es-

*The government of liberty is the despotism of liberty against tyranny.*
—ROBESPIERRE

When the Estates-General convened at Versailles in 1789, Robespierre, a representative from the Artois province, was not the most prominent of the deputies, but his quiet tenacity would soon propel him to the forefront of the French Revolution.

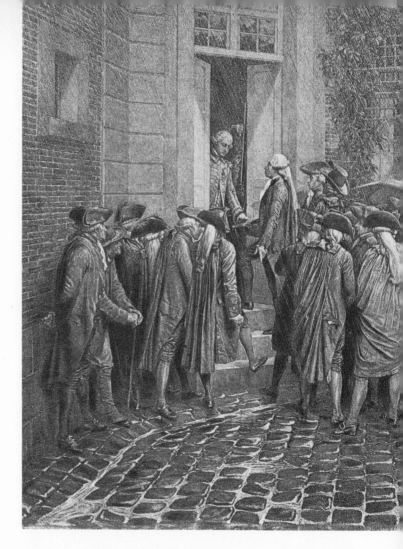

Angered that the Estates-General had transformed itself into the National Assembly, Louis barred the rebellious deputies from their meeting place. Undaunted, the representatives met on the royal tennis court, where they swore to proceed until a constitution was established.

tate, there were some deputies who were willing to modify or surrender some of their privileges. Most wanted to keep them. Those aristocrats who called for reform on a large scale were relatively young. Many were from the cities. Most were familiar with the ideas of the Enlightenment.

Wearing an extravagantly jeweled plumed hat, Louis spoke condescendingly to this gathering. He grandly proclaimed, in his usual bland tones, that he alone commanded France and that "restlessness and an exaggerated desire for change" were being kept under control, thanks to his deputies' good judgment. Then Necker gave a long speech, boring the deputies — especially those in the back of the hall. In this speech he was careful to avoid mentioning what many deputies in the Third Estate

found to be the most obvious stumbling block: that there were three estates rather than one national assembly. Many deputies realized that they would have to unify the Estates-General by themselves. In the succeeding days, the three estates met in separate buildings, with the Third Estate occupying the largest one. Almost at once the commons (and the clergyman Sieyès, who was the leading advocate of the idea) began to pressure the clergy and the nobility to join with them in a single representative body.

The three estates differed on numerous points, but they all recognized that royal absolutism was the greatest obstacle to progress. Other important grievances concerned individual freedoms to say and print what one wished.

Members of the Third Estate decided that they could convince the parish priests to leave the clergy's ranks and join them. It was known that there were major disputes between the older and younger, the richer and poorer priests. This campaign brought Robespierre some recognition among his fellow deputies. On May 28 he made a speech in which he gave the clergy a tongue-lashing. He denounced an archbishop who suggested that the Third Estate come to terms with the clergy and nobility. Robespierre shot back that the archbishop was guilty of "holding up our discussions with spurious delays." He also accused the archbishop and high church officials of being against the poor,

*Fédérés* — volunteer soldiers dedicated to the defense of the revolution — leave the city of Marseilles for Paris, which was the revolution's center. The ongoing turmoil and discontent of the masses ultimately enabled Robespierre and other radical leaders to gain control of the revolution.

charging that church officials accumulated riches while the poor went hungry: "All that is necessary is that the bishops and dignitaries of the church should renounce that luxury which is an offense to Christian humility . . . they should give up their coaches and give up their horses; if need be, that they should sell a quarter of the church property, and give it to the poor." More often than not, however, the other deputies were impatient with Robespierre when he got up to speak. There were no rules of order to prevent them from jeering and heckling.

During this period, Robespierre clearly had little in common with the frequently outrageous Mirabeau. Mirabeau was a colorful figure with a well-

Awe-struck former prisoners are released from the Bastille on July 14, 1789. The date has become France's most important national holiday. The storming of the Bastille and other insurrectionary acts demonstrated that the majority of Parisians were unwilling to settle for moderate or partial reforms.

known past. Robespierre was not. Mirabeau was a massive figure with a huge head, whereas Robespierre stood only a little more than five feet tall and was slight with pinched features. Mirabeau enjoyed sensual pleasures, some said to excess, and he wrote the scandalous *Erotica biblion*. Robespierre, who was certainly no writer of pornography, already demonstrated an abiding concern for morality and virtue and scorned sensual enjoyments as indicating a lack of virtue. When Mirabeau entered the chamber, other deputies drew away in disgust, but he nevertheless commanded their attention whenever he spoke. He was both brilliant and eloquent. As for Robespierre, however, it was reported that on one occasion he was so flustered that he was forced to leave the rostrum in tears. Mirabeau gave more than 100 speeches from 1789 to 1790. Robespierre managed to give fewer than 30.

If his career in the Estates-General was off to a slow start, Robespierre's name and opinions found their way into several radical newspapers, such as *Le Mercure National* and *Le Moniteur*. In fact, even Mirabeau did not ignore his younger, somewhat peevish colleague and published stories in his own newspaper about Robespierre's activities.

Despite their differences, both men thought similarly concerning civic obligations. They agreed that responsibility to the state was necessary in a constitutional republic. Soon, Robespierre joined the radical Breton Club. Among its other 40 charter members were Sieyès, Grégoire, and Mirabeau.

The Third Estate, meanwhile, was gaining ground against the king. Squabbles broke out between the bishops and parish priests. Soon a delegation from the Third Estate asked the clergy to join their ranks "in the name of the God of Peace." Sieyès then proposed that the clergy and nobility join the Third Estate and defy the king. By June 13, a few priests had drifted over to the Third Estate. On June 17, Mirabeau, Sieyès, and Jean-Joseph Mounier succeeded in getting the Third Estate to declare itself the *l'assemblée nationale* — the National Assembly. Two days later, a majority of the clergy voted to join. The motion passed by 491 votes to 89.

Having already lost one bout with the Third Estate over the clergy, Louis decided to lock the deputies out of their meeting place, the *salle des menus plaisirs du roi*. He planned to force them to attend a *séance royale*, or royal session, of the Estates-General. This meeting was to convene on June 22. The ploy did not work. Still defiant, the Third Estate went to the Jeu de Paume, a tennis court, on June 20. There the deputies took a solemn oath ("the tennis court oath") not to recess or adjourn until a constitution was established "on firm foundations." Robespierre was the 45th deputy to sign his name to the oath.

The séance royale was postponed a day, and the Third Estate was able on this occasion to meet with the clergy at an alternative meeting place furnished by the clergy, the Church of Saint Louis. When the deputies strode into the rue de Chantiers on June 23 to meet with the king, Louis insisted that the estates resume their separate status. Such a royal order now carried little weight. Deputies from the Third Estate were given new courage by having won over so many members of the clergy. After the king and the nobles stalked out, the Third Estate stayed where they were, and Mirabeau forcefully told his comrades that they must uphold their oath and resist the king's dictates. It was understood that if any member fell ill, he was to be carried by fellow deputies into the assembly's meetings. As royal troops surrounded the building during Mirabeau's impassioned speech, popular support for the new National Assembly ran high in nearby Paris. Even Robespierre was impressed with Mirabeau's courage and tenacity.

With the population cheering the newly created National Assembly at every turn, Louis did not dare to force the deputies to disperse. Unable to order the body to disband, he capitulated and instructed the clergy and the nobility to merge with the National Assembly on June 27. Ominously, Swiss and German troops in the king's service continued to flow into the area around Paris and Versailles.

Robespierre accompanied a delegation that met with the king in early July to ask him to call off his troops. Louis refused. He was offended by the delegation's suggestion that the soldiers were meant to be a threat rather than a "precaution." Of course, the king was planning to crush unrest and dissolve the National Assembly by force. When it was learned that Louis had dismissed Necker, his only capable financial adviser, shock waves ran through Paris. Stockbrokers closed the stock exchange when prices on treasury notes suddenly dropped. Workers feared that bread prices would rise and guessed correctly that aristocrats were hoarding badly needed grain on their estates in the hope that the nation's poor would turn against the Third Estate. The workers' wages already lagged well behind food prices. Bandits, mainly hungry peasants, had roamed the countryside for many years. Now riots swept through Paris. In order to protect private property,

*I will never consent to the spoliation of my clergy or my nobility. And I will not sanction decrees which seek to despoil them.*

—KING LOUIS XVI
stating his opposition to
The Declaration of the
Rights of Man and Citizen

a group of middle-class Parisians established a militia that soon would become the National Guard. No longer able to contain their rage, peasants pillaged the nobles' estates in the provinces. The period of the peasants' rebellion and the panic it engendered is known as the Great Fear.

On July 14 the Bastille, a prison-fortress in Paris that to many symbolized tyranny, was stormed by a huge mob and some members of the National Guard. The following day, Robespierre was with the crowd that accompanied Louis from Versailles to Paris after he told his soldiers to stop fighting. On July 16 Necker was restored to office, but the damage caused by his dismissal could not be undone. Writing to Buissart, Robespierre recorded his enthusiasm on seeing the king humbled and the Bastille conquered. When the revolution at last took the form of armed revolt, Robespierre commented, "They talk about riots, but this riot, sirs, is freedom."

In his speeches and memoranda Robespierre began to express his belief that opponents of the revolution should be executed, or at least punished, without hesitation. After the governor of the Bastille and the other officials were beheaded by the prison's frenzied attackers, Robespierre demanded that future "suspects" be treated the same way. More mod-

Intoxicated by their new-found freedom, peasants burn feudal titles raided from the castles of their former lords after the National Assembly's 1789 decree abolishing feudalism.

A female figure representing "Equality" holds a tablet inscribed with the Declaration of the Rights of Man and Citizen. The document expressed many ideals of the revolution and proclaimed that "the aim of every political association is the preservation of the natural and undoubted rights of man."

erate speakers wondered how order could be maintained. Robespierre countered that if the people were prevented from avenging themselves upon their enemies, they would think they were being deceived and that the revolution was being betrayed. He attacked the release of one aristocrat who had tried to stop the rebels from seizing a supply of gunpowder.

After the National Assembly voted to abolish the seigneurs' feudal rights on August 4, Robespierre made clear his position on freedom of the press. He was unequivocally for it. During this particular speech he added that each citizen was a "guardian of Freedom" who must be ready to sound the alarm at the slightest rumor of a threat to liberty. Robespierre was noted for his odd speaking style; he spoke in unusually long sentences, and at moments when he paused and his listeners thought he was finished, he suddenly resumed speaking. Such pauses often signaled unexpected changes in meaning.

While violence continued to shake the cities and villages, the Declaration of the Rights of Man and Citizen was proclaimed on August 26. Its first drafts had been written as early as January 1788 by Marie-Joseph du Motier, marquis de Lafayette. (Lafayette, who had previously distinguished himself by helping the Americans in their revolution against the British, was commander of the National Guard from July 1789 until September 1791.) The document was a cornerstone of the French revolutionary government. It was based largely upon the American Declaration of Independence, written by the American revolutionary and U.S. president Thomas Jefferson, who in turn had been inspired by the theories of the 17th-century English philosopher John Locke. Locke wrote that "all men are naturally in . . . a state of perfect freedom to order their actions and dispose of their possessions and persons as they see fit."

Montesquieu was another influential source of the Declaration of the Rights of Man. Both he and Locke agreed that government functioned most fairly and judiciously when governing power was divided among several branches — the concept of separation of powers. Unlike Locke, Montesquieu did not argue that the legislative branch should prevail over the others. Many deputies were interested in these ideas, seeing in them a way to prevent any single group from seizing too much power.

In principle, the Declaration was meant to be a guideline for the revolution. D. M. G. Sutherland explains that in the Declaration, "Liberty was defined to mean any activity which does not harm another," a commonsense formulation. Mirabeau's and Robespierre's ideas were more extreme in that they both required citizens to be actively virtuous. When it was time for the National Assembly to establish a constitution, Robespierre wanted to leave his imprint on it. He believed that the king, if allowed to be part of the government, should not have veto power. Conservative feeling ran counter to this view. Nobles wanted the king to be able to have final veto power as a check on the revolution. A more

> *Experience constantly proves that every man who has power is impelled to abuse it.*
> —MONTESQUIEU
> from *The Spirit of the Laws*

middle-of-the-road solution was to give the king partial, or temporary, veto power. Because Mirabeau argued for this solution, Robespierre began to suspect him of being insufficiently committed to the revolution and interested in finding a comfortable position for himself in the king's government. Robespierre's viewpoint did not win out; so many speakers were ready to address the issue that he was not given a chance to speak. The king was granted temporary veto power.

Still the deputy from Artois kept his eye on the other deputies, especially those more influential than he. Mounier and Gui-Jean-Baptiste Target, for example, were two members of the Third Estate who were very cautious about taking too much power from the king. They tended to side with the nobility and the bishops on the veto question. Robespierre perceived them as half-hearted participants in the revolution, believing that they failed to understand that their political loyalty should coincide with the interests they were elected to represent. Unable to stand firm against Louis's supporters in the National Assembly, these two seemed hopelessly sidetracked.

In a journal entry made during the debates over the constitution, Robespierre referred even to Mirabeau as a "zero." Despite the fact that Mirabeau was a leading member of the radical Breton Club, as were Robespierre and the clergymen Sieyès and Grégoire, Mirabeau's brother sat with the monarchist faction in the assembly. To Robespierre, this was another reason to doubt Mirabeau's integrity.

In discussions concerning the constitution, Robespierre did have some impact. He managed to persuade the assembly to accept his motion that freedom of the press be limited only in cases in which libel was committed. Another modest success concerned taxation under the new state. He struggled over subtle differences in legal language, insisting that "establishing the revenue" was an essential phrase.

By September, Necker was attempting to stabilize the financial situation, which had been made worse by a poor harvest that summer. Camille Desmoulins began to suggest that Queen Marie Antoinette, as

> *Is this blood then so pure that one should so regret to spill it?*
> —ANTOINE BARNAVE
> French revolutionist, defending the violence of the revolution

an Austrian, might use her influence with her brother Emperor Joseph II of Austria, who could dispatch troops to break up the National Assembly. Desmoulins also stated that the king should return to Paris. Tensions ran high in Paris while the king and the deputies continued to stare each other down in Versailles. Louis continued to stall over approving the decree of the Declaration of the Rights of Man and Citizen and the abolition of feudal rights. The so-called Flanders Regiment, on the king's orders, was advancing menacingly toward Versailles. There were rumors that aristocrats were plotting to rise up and restore the monarchy. All France was seething with rumor and hearsay. Back in Paris fearful mobs, hungry for bread, were becoming increasingly angry and impatient with the king. In the Palais Royal, where orators often spoke, a woman called on her fellow Parisians to march on Versailles. On Monday, October 5, about 6,000 women armed with scythes, pikes, knives, or whatever was close at hand marched resolutely through a downpour to Versailles. This strange and unruly procession was led by Stanislas Maillard, self-proclaimed hero of the Bastille.

The next day a drenched and discontented crowd burst in upon the deputies of the National Assembly. Robespierre spoke calmly with Maillard and expressed the belief that the "market women" were correct in claiming that aristocrats were hoarding grain and trying to starve the people. Mirabeau bellowed that the crowd should get out, but they wanted their "little mother Mirabeau," as they called him, to know that bread was the issue for them. They then confronted the king, who promised them bread. When Lafayette arrived with the National Guard, the king said he would recognize the National Guard and the Declaration of the Rights of Man. Lafayette requested that the king be permanently relocated to Paris. Consequently both the royal family and the deputies went to Paris, where they were based in the vicinity of the Tuileries Palace. The king and his family became virtual prisoners of the revolution. By November the National Assembly was headquartered in a nearby riding school, or *manège*.

> *Peace will set us back. . . . We can be regenerated through blood alone.*
> —MANON ROLAND
> radical Girondist

Robespierre noted that the manège was particularly well suited for the National Assembly's deliberations because it was a vast space where ever-present corruption could not be hidden. Here the will of the nation would be heard, and the public interest would be served at last. After the deputies moved to Paris, Robespierre quickly found a residence on the rue Saintonge in a building owned by an acquaintance from his days at the Collège de Louis-le-Grand. The Breton Club made its headquarters on the rue Saint Jacques, above a monastery that housed Dominican priests, who were called Jacobins. Robespierre was pleased to be back in Paris, where he was on familiar ground. Having

been educated there, he had also learned to understand its social makeup.

Robespierre addressed the National Assembly on October 20. He charged that plotting against the revolution was still going on; he implored his fellow deputies to realize that circumstances were desperate, that the revolution was in danger. Throughout this period, rioting caused by food shortages was widespread. It did not seem significant to anyone that a baker was murdered during an outbreak of violence the day after Robespierre spoke.

Robespierre, however, detected foul play behind this by now almost commonplace crime. Before his death, the baker had made several loaves of bread.

In October 1789 irate Parisian women marched on the king's palace at Versailles to protest food shortages. When the women were joined by the National Guard under Lafayette, the king and his family were compelled to return to Paris, where they were held as virtual prisoners of the revolution.

Lafayette fought for republican ideals both in America and France. In 1789 he designed the modern French flag, employing the revolutionary tricolor (white, blue, and red), but his disenchantment with the direction the revolution was taking led him to flee France in 1792.

These loaves were to go to the National Assembly to feed deputies. They were now missing, apparently stolen. Behind this incident Robespierre saw no famished rioter but counterrevolutionary conspirators. In addition, he urged the assembly not to vote for the imposition of martial law, as was being considered. Sending troops to suppress the rioters was not likely to win the trust of the people for the National Assembly. François Buzot, another deputy, thought a special court should be set up to try traitors responsible for the crime and others like it. Robespierre called for a national tribunal to dispense revolutionary justice. The tribunal would concentrate solely on treachery against the revolution, which to Robespierre represented nothing less than freedom itself. His words fell on deaf ears.

That same month the Constitutional Committee, set up by the National Assembly to write a constitution, laid down rules determining who was eligible to run for office and who was eligible to be an elector, based on the amount of taxes an individual paid. The Constitutional Committee also decided to divide the French citizenry into "active" and "passive" citizens. Approximately 3 million Frenchmen were declared passive citizens and thus deprived of the vote. Even the elections for the Estates-General, prior to the revolution, had allowed virtually universal suffrage. The new rules implied that some citizens were part of the "general will" and others were not. Clearly, the Declaration of the Rights of Man and Citizen was not being upheld. Neither the spirit nor the letter of the Declaration was reflected in these rules.

Many radical deputies did not object to the committee's decision. They thought that if the poor and illiterate were granted the right to vote, they would only imitate the more conservative votes of their wealthier peers. Robespierre immediately spoke out against this betrayal of freedom. The state, he believed, was meant to guarantee its citizens more liberty and independence, not diminish their rights. He did not believe that the amount someone paid in taxes should gain him the right to vote, while someone who paid less (because he was poor) could not claim the same right. In his own Artois province, as it turned out, very few individuals would have the right to vote. In order to provide these disenfranchised with the right to vote, Robespierre devised a tax for the poorer farmers in Artois to pay. The tactic provided ammunition for his critics. Certain citizens in Arras fought to destroy Robespierre's credibility. His sister Charlotte, his faithful brother, Augustin, and the new president of Arras's Constitutional Club, Fouché, countered these critics. Despite Robespierre's protests, it was decreed on October 29 that there would be active and passive citizens.

Robespierre continued to receive unfavorable publicity back home in Artois. Journalists there had grown displeased with their arrogant deputy, but Robespierre was no longer concerned with pleasing his provincial critics. His ambition had outgrown being a humble provincial representative. Sure that he was responsible for the revolution's safekeeping, he believed now that he spoke for France as a whole.

> *Stop slandering the people by always representing them as unworthy of enjoying their rights, as if they were wicked, barbarous and corrupt. You are the corrupt ones.*
> —ROBESPIERRE
> speaking before the
> National Convention

# 5

# The Incorruptible

In Paris, Robespierre sat on the left side of the chamber with the National Assembly's radical members, while the conservative deputies were seated on the right. (Their locations formed the basis for the common political labels "left" and "right.") While the people of France became more accustomed to their new government, organizations called *fédérations* sprang up in the provinces. These were established by the provincial communities to celebrate the revolution. A spirit of unity born of the heady days of revolution triumphed over regional disputes.

Governmental authority in France was becoming increasingly decentralized. In some localities municipal government collapsed so suddenly that there was little to take its place. In Paris, the National Assembly began to establish executive as well as legislative functions, initiating policy through various committees. As a result, the parlements were disbanded. The king was offended, his power diminished by revolutionary attacks on what had once been his absolute domain. Many of his powers were

> *[Robespierre] saw where the avenues of persuasion lay, and had an instinct for how parliaments might be led and controlled.*
> —HILAIRE BELLOC
> Robespierre biographer

**Although this 18th-century portrait depicts Robespierre holding a bouquet of flowers and looking like a traditional suitor, the young deputy to the National Assembly was interested more in courting power than women.**

curtailed. Those that he retained were his at the assembly's discretion. Mirabeau repeatedly warned the king to seek reconciliation with the revolutionaries, but Louis was appalled at these suggestions. Deputies who sympathized with the king, such as Mounier, became known as the *monarchiens*, or monarchists. Mounier agitated briefly for the royalist cause in Dauphiné, his home province. They found few who would listen to their message, and many, including Mounier, were forced to leave France.

The revolution based in Paris was rapidly doing away with the ancien régime. Other leading industrial and commercial cities, such as Lyons and Marseilles, were also in revolt, overturning the monarchy's municipal government, while in the countryside feudal institutions were crumbling. Once very centralized, local governments were also toppled. Previously, their word had been law. In fact, the royal bureaucracy had begun falling apart as early as the summer of 1789. In its place sprang up district assemblies whose governmental powers were backed up by Lafayette's National Guard.

**Soldiers and citizens gather outside the headquarters of the Jacobin Club, which elected Robespierre president in 1790. The Jacobins were one of the most powerful and dangerous of the revolutionary societies that sprang up in France during the period.**

The revolution provided opportunities not only for releasing the population's pent-up destructiveness, but also for joyful celebration. Throughout the towns and villages the populace was intoxicated with the revolution's success. Many cashed in on the economic disruption. Nevertheless, although personal freedoms were expanding for those who previously had been little more than serfs (agricultural servants bound to the land), not everyone was happy. Farmland owned by the clergy was nationalized. The wealthy from both the middle classes and the aristocracy were beginning to leave France, taking their riches with them. In the confusion, peasants from the smaller towns intercepted grain shipments bound for large cities such as Lyons, causing city dwellers, who had suffered from the disastrous harvest of 1788, to experience further hardship. To combat the continuing problem of state bankruptcy and to raise revenues with which to run the government, state bonds called *assignats* were issued in December of 1789. These assignats rapidly became the currency of revolutionary France. In late 1790 there were more than 1 billion assignats in circulation throughout the country.

These measures were still not sufficient to correct French economic difficulties. On July 12, 1790, two days before the *fête de la Fédération,* a festival celebrating the first anniversary of the fall of the Bastille, the Civil Constitution of the Clergy was enacted. Under it, church jurisdiction was reorganized according to the pattern set by the government. Priests were required to swear loyalty to the new constitution, causing the clergy to be divided between those who would take the oath and those who would not. Months earlier various religious orders had been banned, except those that performed charitable or educational activities. Robespierre spoke in favor of the constitution, declaring, "When virtue is departed from most individuals you will find it in the corporate existence of the people."

On March 31, 1790, Robespierre was elected president of what now was called the Jacobin Club — formerly the Breton Club. Robespierre's leadership held the Jacobins together. Another political club

*When you undertake to run a revolution, the difficulty is not how to make it go; it is how to hold it in check.*
—COMTE DE MIRABEAU
leading member of the
National Convention

Radical journalist Jean-Paul Marat was known as "the People's Friend," which was also the name of the newspaper he used to launch a series of vicious attacks on government authorities.

was the Cordeliers, founded in April. They were supporters of the radical journalists Jean-Paul Marat and Louis-Marie Fréron, who attacked both Lafayette and Jean-Sylvain Bailly, the mayor of Paris, for having too much power. They also criticized the policy that created active and passive citizens. Similar clubs were mushrooming throughout France. In Lyons and the province of Bordeaux active citizens organized patriotic clubs to protect and expand individual liberties, both for themselves and citizens not yet enfranchised.

Shortly after the election, Robespierre began participating in debates over the new judicial system. He repeated his previous arguments, urging the need for special courts to try political criminals. This time, he proposed that members of the revolutionary courts be popularly elected. For the most part, he got his way, and the subsequent Revolutionary Tribunal clearly reflected many of his recommendations.

Previously, Mirabeau and Robespierre had disagreed over a proposal made by the Constitutional Committee concerning the districts into which Paris, the heart of the revolution, was divided. There was a movement to draw up new political boundaries and reduce the 60 districts already in existence and create 48 "sections" in their place. Mirabeau was for these changes; Robespierre wanted these districts to be regarded as permanent, kept as they were. The debate was a rare instance in which Robespierre received the support of the more conservative deputies. To him, keeping Paris's political boundaries as they were meant preserving the city's radicalism. Conservatives hoped, on the other hand, that maintaining the districts would eventually bring a backlash against the radicals. Robespierre was convinced that the districts were vital to the revolution. The revolution, after all, originally sprang from these districts, he said. He and his unaccustomed allies lost to Mirabeau, and the division of Paris into sections went ahead.

By this time, Robespierre's devotion to the revolution could not be questioned. Even Mirabeau marveled at his zeal. Robespierre placed the revolution's ideals before all else, even personal interests, causing him to become known as "the Incorruptible." He was now more determined than ever to defeat his adversary, Mirabeau, whose motives he regarded as less than pure. Although Robespierre had earlier insisted that once the National Assembly enacted a policy, it was never to be criticized, he did exactly that in order to get at Mirabeau. In a speech he alluded to the fact that Mirabeau was establishing closer personal ties with the king while at the same time trying to pin the blame for counterrevolutionary activities on the prince of Condé.

In December 1790, during debates over restructuring the National Guard, Robespierre heatedly explained that militancy was important to the revolution. Mirabeau, on the contrary, felt that peace between the king and the masses should be established as soon as possible. This meant that membership in the National Guard would be restricted to only the middle classes or reasonably suc-

*[E]verybody knew how to command but nobody knew how to obey.*
—JEAN-SYLVAIN BAILLY
first mayor of Paris
(1789–91)

cessful artisans. Robespierre made himself the spokesman for the passive citizens, who in the large towns were essentially the sans-culottes. No one else, it seems, was willing to speak up on their behalf in the assembly, which rendered them politically as well as economically disadvantaged.

Marat commented that Robespierre grew pale at the sight of a sword, but he lifted his voice with unusual passion to defend revolutionary violence. He defended the passive citizens' occasional disruptiveness; he scoffed at those who seemed to think that revolution could be made without "disturbances." Mirabeau and his supporters were doing nothing less than depriving the people of the rights for which the revolution was being fought.

Robespierre's searing speech caused Mirabeau almost physical pain. When the accuser finished his address, the stunned Mirabeau saw that he was left with the support of but a few stragglers, while the elfin Robespierre was nearly hidden by his new, hard-won supporters. Mirabeau spent the remaining months of his life in close contact with the king and his advisers, dying in April 1791 at age 42.

In February 1791 the first bishops of the church were elected according to the strictures of the Civil Constitution of the Clergy. These impositions on the church were not well received by the populace as a whole. Priests who refused to recognize the Civil Constitution of the Clergy took to the streets in protest wearing white cockades, or decorative badges,

**Freedom fighter Toussaint L'Ouverture (center) leads a 1791 slave uprising in the French colony of Haiti. Robespierre argued that slavery should be abolished in French colonies in accordance with the egalitarian ideals of the revolution.**

on their hats that signified that their wearers were sympathetic to the king. Priests who refused to take the required oath under the constitution were forced to leave their parishes and their villages, often in the wake of street violence. Soon the head of the Catholic church, Pope Pius VI, condemned the constitutional reorganization of the clergy in France. His opposition only fanned the flames of unrest.

The revolution's supporters often wore soft red "liberty caps" and took snuff from snuff boxes bearing the revolutionary blue, white, and red. The word "feudal" came to be used humorously with reference to anything that was old-fashioned or no longer worked. Noble titles such as "marquis" and "count," which were feudal in origin, were deemed impermissible since their abolition in June of the previous year.

Remaining opposed to the electoral laws, which to him were unjust, Robespierre, in April, presented his views before the Cordelier Club, a disorderly group compared with the Jacobins. (By now the Jacobins had several hundred affiliated clubs throughout the provinces. The greatest unrest and turmoil with respect to government policies usually occurred in areas where the Jacobins' influence was strongest.) Many members of the Cordeliers were passive citizens, and they wildly approved of what Robespierre had to say.

Not long afterward, the National Assembly, or Constituent Assembly as it was increasingly called, had to contend with the question of the French slave trade. Robespierre found himself up against the assembly's three strongest deputies, Adrien Duport, Alexandre Lameth, and Joseph Barnave. This formidable trio belonged to the Massiac Club, the sole purpose of which was to maintain the slave trade. Robespierre belonged to an organization that opposed slavery. The Constituent Assembly, however, did not grant equal rights and freedom to black slaves in French colonial territories in Africa. It was still thought that slavery was too vital to France's economic interests to eliminate.

Perhaps prophetically, Mirabeau had said shortly

> *The bravest are the best and an excess of firmness is the safeguard of the body. We amputate the gangrened limb to save the rest of the body.*
> —MAXIMIN ISNARD
> member of the Legislative Assembly, speaking in support of a war against counterrevolutionaries

Louis XVI and his family are held captive by revolutionary soldiers at the home of a grocer in Varennes following an unsuccessful attempt in June 1791 to escape from Paris, the stronghold of the revolution.

before his death that he was taking the "last shreds" of the French monarchy with him. He had once advised the king to seek refuge in Rouen, in Normandy, even if a civil war broke out as a result. Animosity toward the king mounted in Paris, and when he and the royal family asked to take Holy Communion on Easter at St. Cloud on April 18, 1791, they were turned down. In dismay, Louis ventured outside the palace and was shocked by the sight that greeted him — milling, cursing crowds, National Guardsmen on horseback. The royal family resolved that night to escape from the palace. Louis and Marie Antoinette agreed that June 20 would be the day of their getaway. They planned to take carriages by night to Montmédy in Lorraine, where they would meet the royalist Marquis de Biollé and his troops. The marquis and his soldiers would form an escort. If they made their escape, the queen was

sure that her second brother, Leopold II, the emperor of Austria, would use his troops to intimidate the National Assembly and make the revolutionaries renegotiate the king's powers.

Accordingly, on June 20 the royal family set out, but their disappearance was discovered the following day. Lafayette sent out an order declaring that "enemies of the revolution" had taken the king and that he was to be restored to the National Assembly's custody at once. Louis and his family were apprehended in the town of Varennes, where they tried to hide, and were returned, as if they were prized fugitives, to the Tuileries Palace on June 25.

Meanwhile on May 18, one month after the king had been refused his journey to St. Cloud, Robespierre spoke before the Constituent Assembly. What he had to say was extremely unsettling. Two days earlier discussions had opened concerning creating

Following their unsuccessful escape attempt, the royal
family is escorted past some of Paris's bedraggled poor
as they enter the Constituent Assembly. The question of
what to do with Louis divided France's leaders as the
revolution escalated.

a new legislative body. A key issue was who would run for this legislature and what would be their qualifications. The Constitutional Committee's recommendations were enthusiastically received.

On the 18th, Robespierre quite flatly told his audience that when new elections were held, none of those present should be reelected. In effect, he was calling for an end to his own and his colleagues' roles in the revolution as deputies. Those deputies seated on the right once again thought that possibly Robespierre was correct. It was not, however, a significant sacrifice for them to lose their deputyships because most were already certain they stood no chance of being reelected. Others protested that without the present deputies there would be no one with experience to guide the new representatives when they took office.

Robespierre devised an interesting and clever response to this argument. Knowing that the ancient Roman statesmen were revered by the assembly's members, he told them to envision themselves as sacrificing their personal interests for the good of the constitution. Act as the Romans would have acted when their patriotic duty was presented to them, he urged them. He appealed to their desire for greatness as well as their wish to uphold the constitution. Furthermore, those who would take their places would have as much experience in continuing the revolution as those whom they succeeded had had in starting it. In any event, France would go on without them. There were some further objections, but Robespierre parried each in its turn. There also were no interruptions, unlike his speeches at Versailles. His audience remained silent, captivated by his well-developed logic. One of his most bitter antagonists, Duport, asked whether Robespierre believed the revolution should go on indefinitely, thus inviting a possible dictatorship. Robespierre made no reply. Though disappointing to some, his silence was wiser than a rash answer. To Desmoulins, he proved himself to be a true patriot. Robespierre carried the day: the new Legislative Assembly would consist of all newly elected members.

# 6

# "He Who Trembles Is Guilty"

In the summer of 1791 tensions increased as the assembly tightened its control over political clubs. In June restrictions on workers' guilds and the closing of workshops had caused workers to stage demonstrations. One such demonstration, which included the Cordelier Club, was held at the Champ de Mars on July 17. The participants, some of whom were armed, became violent and hostile. Lafayette's National Guard became frightened and began shooting. Perhaps 50 demonstrators were killed. The Cordelier Club was closed until August 7. Radicals, such as the journalist Jacques René Hébert and Desmoulins, were arrested.

That July, while the workers were under increasing pressure from the National Assembly, Robespierre had published another pamphlet, entitled "Address of Maximilien Robespierre to the French." Although within the Jacobin Club there was considerable argument and disagreement, Robespierre's popularity was on the rise in the

> *It is to be feared that the Revolution, like Saturn, will end by devouring its own children.*
> —PIERRE VERGNIAUD
> president of the Legislative Assembly

**In many of his public addresses, Robespierre characterized himself as an isolated idealist who stood alone against a rising tide of corruption and treachery within the revolutionary government. In reality, he was a master orchestrator of the machinery that meted out "justice" during the French Revolution.**

Parisians gather at the Champ de Mars in 1791 to commemorate the second anniversary of the storming of the Bastille. Robespierre, who came to the festival to circulate a petition demanding that the king be put on trial, narrowly escaped death after National Guardsmen opened fire on the celebrants.

countryside. His rival Barnave finally broke with the Jacobins and formed the Feuillant Club. (In addition to these organizations, various patriotic societies sprang up in Bordeaux, Lyons, and other localities around France.) Only a handful of Jacobin groups, however, deserted Robespierre. He was careful in his pamphlet to distance himself from the government's recent policies against workers' coalitions and from the massacre at the Champ de Mars. "I have always held that equality of rights belongs to all members of the state, that the nation includes the working class, and everyone," he wrote. He described himself as a "simple, weak, isolated individual" against enemies armed with "money, slander . . . bayonets."

On the day of the massacre, the Jacobins were holding a meeting. After the massacre, anyone who could be linked to the riot was subject to arrest. When Robespierre left the hall he was approached by a man named Maurice Duplay, a master carpenter, who admired the Jacobin leader. Duplay was a new member of the club. He offered Robespierre lodging at his home until the panic subsided. His host's hospitality was so winning that the house on rue Saint Honoré became Robespierre's new home. Duplay's entire family greatly impressed Robespierre, and the family virtually idolized him.

In September the king reluctantly approved the new constitution. The departing deputies completed their final legislative act by passing a "self-denying ordinance." Another phase in the French Revolution was about to get underway. When the Legislative Assembly convened for the first time on October 1, a new revolutionary movement began, just as Robespierre wanted. Few nobles or members of the clergy were elected this time; the new assembly was comprised mainly of middle-class members. This new generation of revolutionaries was brought together largely under the *Girondins*, or *Girondists*.

**A mob storms a printer's shop to obtain the latest issues of revolutionary newspapers in a satiric engraving entitled "Freedom of the Press." Throughout the revolution, journalists such as Marat stirred up the citizens of France with false allegations and violent rhetoric.**

The Girondists took their name from the region called the Gironde, one of the 83 *départements*, or political regions, recently established. They were led by the patriot and editor of *La Patriote français*, Jacques-Pierre Brissot. Brissot was extremely idealistic, dedicated to Rousseau's least practical doctrines. He and the Girondists believed that they could retain the monarchy as part of the government, with the middle and more wealthy classes ensuring that the king did not overstep his bounds. Brissot also thought that the French Revolution was simply the first in a series that would overthrow the monarchies that ruled Europe.

Having regained certain official functions when he accepted the constitution, the king used his veto power (which was never abolished) against the Girondists. Led by Brissot, the Girondists demanded that the *emigrés*, those who had fled France to escape the revolution, be returned and their whereabouts revealed. The city of Koblenz, along the Rhine River in western Germany, was becoming a base for emigré counterrevolutionary operations under the command of the duke of Brunswick, Karl Wilhelm Ferdinand. When in November the king vetoed the decree demanding the return of the

emigrés, Brissot declared that all tyranny would be smashed by French revolutionary troops. Brissot proclaimed in December that the French people must go to war as soon as possible in order to export the revolution. "The French people will utter a great shout and all the other peoples will reply," he stated. With his war cries, Brissot set the tone for the Legislative Assembly.

In January 1792, Robespierre, as leader of the Jacobin Club, told the Legislative Assembly that Brissot was mistakenly assuming that revolutionary fervor could triumph over the armies of Austria and Prussia. Robespierre said this was as absurd as putting swords in missionaries' hands. They would meet only with resistance. Although Brissot was silenced that day, his newspaper was not, and it began to vilify Robespierre, hinting that perhaps he was an Austrian spy.

On January 14 Brissot gave an ultimatum to Leopold II of Austria. He arrogantly demanded that Leopold immediately reaffirm an old peace treaty between Austria and France. Clearly, Brissot was trying to start a war. Russia, Austria, and Prussia knew that France was militarily weak at this time, and that with France vanquished it would be easier

This caricature depicts members of the French aristocracy making the best of their plight by playing cards and gossiping during their imprisonment in the Conciergerie fortress.

A French soldier drags off a wounded comrade during the War of the First Coalition, fought by France against Prussia and Austria. Robespierre opposed the Girondist majority in the Legislative Assembly, who believed that a war would liberate Europe from its tyrannical monarchies.

to resume partitioning Poland among themselves. In the meantime, Robespierre found an unwanted ally in Marat, whose writings in the newspaper *L'Ami du peuple (The Friend of the People)* attacked almost everyone, it seemed, except the sans-culottes. He was a man said to have embodied the Terror before there was such a policy. Marat considered the Girondists' motives suspect. In his opinion the massacre at the Champ de Mars was justification for brutal reprisals. This physically repellent, unpleasant man visited Robespierre to express his admiration for the Jacobin leader and his contempt for the *propagandistes de guerre* (war propagandists). Robespierre did not much care for Marat, but he agreed with him concerning the issue of war. He was astounded by how bloodthirsty Marat was, however, and soon showed his guest the door.

On January 25 the Legislative Assembly issued a decree saying that if the Austrians did not reply to its ultimatum in 10 days, war would be declared. Leopold died on March 1. His successor, Francis II, refused to be cowed by Brissot's saber rattling. He was willing to fight, and he formed an alliance with the Prussians.

The French king was then being maneuvered by the Girondists to declare war. Brissot was prevented by the constitution from putting members of the Legislative Assembly on the king's cabinet. Instead, the Girondist sympathizers Jean Marie Roland and Charles François Dumouriez, a soldier with a craving for power, were appointed to key cabinet positions. Robespierre disapproved of both Dumouriez and Roland. Dumouriez was a buffoon who thought his clumsy jokes would soften Robespierre's dislike for the Girondist ministers. Dumouriez's attempt at forcing a red liberty cap onto Robespierre's head, for example, proved an awkward mistake. The sansculottes were becoming more and more restless, caring little for the arguments between the Feuillants, Girondists, and Jacobins.

The Girondists cleverly exploited the people's fear that the Prussians and the Austrians would unite to restore the full power of the French monarchy. Louis declared war on April 20, 1792. He was convinced that his decision would boost his popularity, but the ensuing War of the First Coalition only brought his doom that much closer.

The war, fought in the Austrian Netherlands (present-day Belgium), got off to a bad start for France. The revolutionary troops were in disarray. Distrust for officers was so intense that one French commander, General Théobald Dillon, was murdered by his own troops.

At home the monarchy was again under siege. After Louis dismissed his cabinet ministers on June 12, anger against the king mounted, and on June 20 a mob of 8,000 people shouting "No aristocrats! No veto! No priests!" burst into the Tuileries Palace, menacing and mocking the king. It was the third anniversary of the tennis court oath.

When Lafayette returned from the front to Paris on June 28, it appeared that the Girondists and Robespierre could at least agree in their contempt for the man they considered the villain responsible for the Champ de Mars. In front of the Legislative Assembly, Lafayette spoke against the Jacobins. By late August, the proud general would defect to the Austrian side.

Citizen soldiers open fire on the heavily guarded Tuileries Palace on August 10, 1792. By the day's end, the frightened royal family had taken refuge in the assembly building, and over 500 of the king's guards had been slain.

The royal family listens from behind a window as the Legislative Assembly debates their fate. The day after the storming of the Tuileries, the assembly decided to offer the king its protection, but this promise proved meaningless in the volatile political climate of the revolution.

Brissot and Robespierre quickly resumed their public attacks on each other. On one occasion Desmoulins shouted that Brissot was a scoundrel. Brissot angrily rejected Robespierre's followers' suggestion that Brissot and the king were political allies. While the two leaders abused each other in their speeches, Robespierre began publishing a newspaper called *Le Défenseur de la Constitution* (*The Defender of the Constitution*). Its publication ceased in 1793.

In late July the Brunswick manifesto, named for the duke of Brunswick, set another crisis in motion. The duke threatened that his Prussian and Austrian forces would invade Paris unless the king was restored to full authority. This threat was made just as 20,000 *fédérés* (volunteer soldiers) were streaming toward Paris from Brest and Marseilles for the Festival of the Federation.

Robespierre hoped that the crises at home would develop into a full-fledged uprising that would save the revolutionary state. Impatient to see the revolt materialize, he declared, "Nothing is unconstitutional except that which leads to its [the state's] ruin."

It was evident that Brissot's followers were using the king as a way to control the revolution. Robespierre could no longer show any doubt or hesitation about what was to be done with the monarchy. A republic must be set up in its place, he decided. In previous meetings with the Jacobins he had fidgeted and expressed skepticism whenever there was talk about making France into a republic. He sometimes cut off speakers in midsentence by asking, "What is a republic?" He now believed there was no other choice.

In August, Robespierre envisaged the next stage in the revolution. First, the king must be overthrown. Next, a new ruling body must be elected to replace the Legislative Assembly. This was to be the National Convention. Again, no one from the previous assembly would serve on the new one. In addition, the National Convention would be elected by universal suffrage. The right to vote would no longer be restricted to active citizens. The National Convention's first task would be to draft a new, more radical constitution than that of 1791.

That month several events brought Robespierre's plans closer to realization. Petitions from all 48 sections of Paris except one agreed that Louis must be deposed. Robespierre was encouraged. He wrote his friend and future colleague on the Committee of Public Safety, Georges Couthon: "The Sections of Paris reveal an energy and wisdom worthy to serve as a model for the rest of the state." By August 9, the Paris Insurrectionary Commune had emerged, built by the "active" citizens, who feared that their rights and interests were being threatened by the Legislative Assembly. This group overthrew the original Paris Commune, which had been the city's revolutionary government since June 1789. Robespierre became the representative for his section but attended meetings for only a brief period. His primary goal was to organize elections for the National Convention.

On August 10, the day after the Insurrectionary Paris Commune was formed, the fédérés and the sans-culottes stormed the Tuileries Palace and massacred about 900 of the king's Swiss Guards.

**Popular leader Georges-Jacques Danton was one of Robespierre's most powerful rivals. A bold opportunist, he was ultimately toppled by the virtuous and singleminded Robespierre.**

Revolutionary officials separate King Louis XVI from his son, the would-be heir to the throne. The boy eventually died in prison in 1795. The king was tried in late 1792 and sentenced to death as an enemy of the people.

Guards who were not killed during the riot were later beheaded on a guillotine set up at the entrance to the palace. Louis, stripped of his remaining power, was imprisoned.

Robespierre refused to sit on a new tribunal created to try and execute those who had fought for the king. Georges-Jacques Danton, a leading member of the Cordelier Club, was appointed minister of justice, while the Girondists regained their cabinet positions. A massive figure with a personality that matched his great physical strength, Danton invited Robespierre to join the judiciary committee he headed. Robespierre declined, though the two revolutionaries were not yet the enemies they later became. Danton was a dominant influence at this time. Previously, he had held only a minor post, beginning in 1791, with the first Paris Commune. An assignment Robespierre did accept was to try to enlist the mayor of Paris's support against counterrevolutionaries. The mayor remained unmoved by Robespierre's arguments and was later defeated by Robespierre in elections to the National Convention on September 5.

Chaos reigned during the weeks prior to the election for the National Convention. In the last days of August, the duke of Brunswick's forces entered France. On August 23 the French were defeated by the Prussian army at Longwy. Verdun fell to the Prussians on September 2. Reports of loyalist uprisings in the Vendée (a department in western France), along with the military peril, threw Danton into a frenzy to unify the people against foreign and internal enemies. With Marat's gleeful encouragement, about 1,000 Parisians went on a rampage. Prisoners were dragged from the jails and killed as traitors. "Let the blood of the traitors flow," Marat said. Although Robespierre said nothing disapproving about this slaughter, he did say that the people's enemies were not yet crushed and that Brissot was in league with the duke of Brunswick. When Verdun was surrendered to the Prussians, Danton exclaimed, "We must dare, and dare, and dare again — and France is saved!" On September 20, Dumouriez and General Francois Kellermann managed to drive back the Prussians at Valmy in the Argonne forest. On the same day, the National Convention met in Paris. The following day the monarchy was abolished, and on September 22 the French Republic was declared. According to the revolutionary calendar, inaugurated with the declaration of the Republic, it was now the Year One.

The National Convention, the third ruling body since 1789, was more radical and represented more of the poor and middle classes than even the previous Legislative Assembly. The most radical deputies, including the Cordeliers and the Jacobins, sat furthest to the left and came to be called the Montagnards, or the Mountain, so called because they occupied the highest seats. To the right were the Girondists. Between these two was a large, undecided majority, referred to as the Plain. Among the delegates was Robespierre's soon-to-be close associate Couthon, who was confined to a wheelchair. Robespierre also met the infamous Louis de

**The deposed king, Louis XVI, approaches the guillotine on January 21, 1793. The ineffective ruler had perhaps his finest hour as he faced death bravely and expressed the vain hope that he would be the last to die for the French Republic.**

A woman from the rebellious Vendée region picks up a gun to defend her family as soldiers search for "traitors of the revolution." The Girondist war with Austria and Prussia inspired revolt in many parts of France.

Saint-Just, who became his closest follower. Saint-Just's fanatical devotion to the coming revolutionary purges earned him the nickname "The Angel of Death." To the Girondists, Robespierre, Danton, and Marat (who also won a seat in the National Convention) were dangerous opponents. Girondist supporters from the provinces frequently demonstrated nearby during meetings of the National Convention, demanding the heads of these three.

The National Convention was in session for only a few days before Robespierre came under attack. A deputy from Marseilles accused him, point-blank, of plotting to create a dictatorship. In reply, Robespierre asserted that France must remain a unified republic in order to ensure its own survival. His opponents, he said, were guilty of wanting to establish separate republics within France, thus causing the nation to become more vulnerable to its enemies. Robespierre made those who denounced him appear to be endangering France. Their ideas would, if put into action, place the Republic in jeopardy.

Many deputies from the provinces found Robespierre's words to their liking. He was actually trying to dispel the hostility felt in the countryside for Paris. Later, tightening his grip on the Jacobin Club, he spoke against "criminal" factions and intriguers in the National Convention. The doors of the Jacobin Club were closed to Brissot and his followers. More denunciations came Robespierre's way in the National Convention. A speaker for the Girondists charged that Robespierre could take no credit for the assault on the king's palace in August. Rather, he could only be blamed for the executions at the prison that had followed. His accuser said that Robespierre had instigated these atrocities and was also responsible for aiming to make himself a dictator. Was it possible, his critics asked, that Robespierre was the only true defender of the republic?

Robespierre responded to these charges on November 5, the day before the French victory at Jemappes in the Austrian Netherlands. Denying any role in the September massacres, he said that illegal atrocities and repressive measures used to sustain the revolution could not be condemned unless the revolution itself could be condemned. There could have been no revolution without the breaking of laws. If he had wanted to be a dictator, he would not then have helped create the National Convention. His speech achieved the desired result. He left the floor with applause ringing throughout the manège. Surrounded by the applauding deputies, the Girondists shrank in their seats with fear.

In the closing days of 1792, Louis was at last put on trial before the National Assembly as an enemy of the people. The Girondists tried to defend Louis. It was evident, nevertheless, that as long as Louis lived, his very existence posed the threat of royalist conspiracies against the revolution. Danton, who at first hoped that the king could be spared and deported, finally conceded that "The only place to strike Kings is on the head." Robespierre was adamant. He claimed that the storming of the Tuileries Palace in August was proof enough regarding the people's sentiments toward the king and the monarchy. To him, the main thing was to persuade the National Convention to dispose of the monarch.

*No republican will ever be brought to believe that in order to set 25 million men free, one man must die, that, in order to destroy the office of King, the man who fills it must be killed.*
—JACQUES-PIERRE BRISSOT
French Revolutionary leader, arguing against imposing the death penalty on Louis XVI

Charlotte Corday murdered Jean-Paul Marat for his part in the downfall of the Girondists. Corday killed the journalist in his bathtub, where he spent much of his time to soothe a painful skin condition.

On January 16 a vote was taken, and Danton cast his vote for the death sentence. Robespierre claimed that the same feeling that had once caused him to argue for outlawing the death penalty was the same one that now caused him to vote for Louis's execution. The Montagnards obediently voted to execute the king. A few Girondists rose to the occasion and tried unsuccessfully to block the sentence. Louis went to the guillotine on January 21. Robespierre did not witness the execution; he remained indoors that day, working.

There was little to prevent Robespierre now from seeing plots and counterrevolutionaries almost everywhere. No longer needing to use these hidden foes to defend himself against accusers, they became a weapon with which to torment his opponents.

In February and March the war intensified. France declared war on England, Holland, and Spain and annexed Monaco. Within France, suspicion and mistrust persisted. Certain that Dumouriez planned to reinstate the monarchy, Marat warned that the general was not to be trusted. Militarily the situation began to look bleak for France when Dumouriez's army was battered by the Austrians at the Battle of Neerwinden on March 18. The offensive in Holland was beginning to crumble. Danton was dispatched with another deputy to the Austrian Netherlands to investigate. As it turned out, Dumouriez was beginning negotiations of his own with the Austrians. Robespierre was amazed when Danton spoke reassuringly about Dumouriez before the National Convention. The Girondists stubbornly defended the general, who then confirmed the suspicions against him by defecting to Austria in early April. Meanwhile, a royalist uprising was in progress in the Vendée.

Two days before Dumouriez's treasonous act was revealed, Brissot's *Le Patriote français* had published embarrassingly favorable words about the general. Robespierre began relentlessly hammering at the Girondists once more. "Factions" (implying the Girondists) threatened the Republic from within, he claimed, while war threatened it from without. Girondist crimes, he declared, included giving financial backing to Dumouriez and trying to discredit the Insurrectionary Paris Commune.

In mid-March, Marat was targeted by the Girondists. He was arraigned before the feared Revolutionary Tribunal, which had been established earlier that month. Despised even by the Montagnards, Marat was a devilish opponent when cornered. He also enjoyed the support of the *Enragés*, an exceedingly radical movement that had gained support. Marat won acquittal without much difficulty and was carried aloft by a cheering mob.

Robespierre was not enthusiastic about redistributing income and land, which the Enragés and the sans-culottes were demanding. Yet by early May the Jacobins, partly in an effort to placate the Enragés, instituted price controls called the *maximum*. That same month, the Insurrectionary Committee of the Paris Commune was instituted, providing another avenue through which the Enragés could further influence the National Convention. On May 29 the Girondists were toppled. The Enragés and the sans-culottes had kept up a steady clamoring for the overthrow of the Girondist Committee of 12, which had recently been set up to investigate the Insurrectionary Paris Commune. On May 31 the Girondists were

Queen Marie Antoinette pleads her case before the Revolutionary Tribunal in October 1793. The queen was suspect on two counts: she had been born in Austria, a nation at war with France, and the extravagance of her court had made her a symbol of the hated aristocracy.

thrust before the Committee of Public Safety, which had been formed in April to safeguard the revolution and was presided over by Danton. Robespierre now would see his troublesome adversaries brought to what he considered justice.

During this period, the constitution of 1793 was taking shape under the stewardship of the Jacobin Marie Jean Hérault de Séchelles. The original draft for the constitution had been submitted by Condorcet in February. His plan was rejected in favor of Séchelles's version, which was later approved by the National Convention on June 24.

The Girondists' fall set off a dizzying chain of events. The National Guard occupied strategic points throughout Paris. On June 2 the National Guard and armed citizens forced their way into the hall of the National Convention and remained on hand to see that the 29 key Girondists were expelled. By now Robespierre and the Jacobins were beginning to command enormous power. The Girondists' humiliation did not please their provincial supporters, who were provoked to violence.

Robespierre's suggested additions to the Declaration of the Rights of Man and Citizen reflect his attitude toward the Girondists: "Those who make war on a people to arrest the progress of liberty, and to destroy the rights of man deserve to be attacked by all, not as ordinary citizens, but as brigands, rebels, and assassins."

On July 13 Marat was murdered by a Girondist sympathizer, Charlotte Corday. Despite Marat's energetic contributions to fighting the Girondists, Robespierre was disgusted when he was mourned as a martyr to the revolution. Marat was also a hero to the Enragés, who were also harsh critics of the Committee of Public Safety. Following Marat's assassination, Robespierre joined Couthon, Saint-Just, and Séchelles on the committee on July 27, replacing Danton as its president. Under Robespierre, the committee would eventually engineer Danton's destruction, but at the time Robespierre's rival seemed far from defeat, having been elected president of the National Convention on July 25. (Robespierre's own brief role as its president ended on June 19.)

*Love of country cannot exist when there is neither pity nor love for one's fellow countrymen but only a soul dried up and withered by self-adulation.*
—CAMILLE DESMOULINS
French Revolutionary
leader, protesting
Robespierre's Reign of Terror

With Marat gone, the journalist Hébert emerged to fill the void left by the audacious extremist. His followers, the Hébertists, became Robespierre's next foes. This new political battle began while the economy continued to suffer from shortages and hoarding. The maximum was to no avail in an economy under siege. A British naval blockade bottled up French ships in their ports. Trade was brought to a standstill.

Believing he had been ill treated by the Jacobins, Hébert presented himself to Paris as the new guardian against corruption. His sweeping program called for cracking down on suspects, trying the queen, and ridding the military of aristocrats. Followers of both Hébert and Danton wanted the Committee of Public Safety to take on more tasks and responsibilities. Under this pressure, the committee extended its control over the state. Danton resisted having anything more to do with the committee, although he urged it to expand its work. Couthon, Séchelles, and Saint-Just were frequently away from Paris on various assignments, and their absence left Robespierre to become the vital link between the National Convention and the busy committee. In September the committee was joined by the more extremist supporters of the left: Jean-Nicolas Billaud-Varenne and Jean-Marie Collot d'Herbois. The only moderate on the committee was the engineer Lazare Carnot, who quarreled bitterly with Saint-Just.

Danton's vast popularity proved to be no match for the hardened extremists who were Robespierre's underlings on the committee. Danton, however, wanted the revolutionary government to be forcefully imposed on the provinces for as long as the war was prosecuted. More and more tasks were heaped upon the committee. There were now *comités de surveillance* (surveillance committees), which closely tracked foreigners' movements and activities. Thus, Danton played a significant role in initiating the Reign of Terror, which Robespierre so expertly conducted and which would ultimately devour Danton himself.

The Terror also stemmed from the vociferous Hébertists, who on September 5 descended on the Na-

Georges-Jacques Danton stares defiantly at the crowd as he prepares to mount the scaffold. Although he had been defeated by Robespierre, he remained unbowed. His last words were directed to the executioner. "Show my head to the people," he declared, "it's worth a look!"

An artist's rendering of Charles André Merda's account of the events following the arrest of Robespierre on July 26. Merda claimed that he shot Robespierre while fighting off his would-be rescuers.

tional Convention and agitated for an armed populace. Many Hébertists also infiltrated the Jacobins, who were then insisting that the Terror was the only way to save the Republic. That month the Law of Suspects was passed. Dossiers on suspects were compiled, and the subjects were watched. Ordinary citizens, guilty perhaps of only the pettiest offenses, were singled out as criminals against the state. The Committee of Public Safety and the guillotine performed the Terror's gruesome labors with savage vigor from October 1793 until March 1794, when Robespierre saw the 18 leading Hébertists sentenced to death. Marie Antoinette was beheaded on October 16. She was followed by Bailly, former mayor of Paris, and by Barnave, Robespierre's rival from his days in the Legislative Assembly.

The decision to arrest Danton was reached on March 30, 1794, at a joint meeting of the Committee of Public Safety and the less powerful Committee of General Security. Robespierre's animosity for Danton was well known. During March their mutual contempt began to boil over. Danton dared to mock Robespierre's principle of virtue, which was as sacred to him as his belief in the Supreme Being, and his dislike for atheists such as Hébert. It also appeared to Robespierre increasingly odd that Danton had taken the committee's side against the Hébertists. Robespierre began stalking the Dantonists. He suspected that Danton's real motive was to undermine the Committee of Public Safety by encouraging a struggle with the Hébertists. The last time they saw each other was at a play, only days before Danton's arrest. Danton shook his mighty fist at the pale figure in the balcony, who faintly waved back for the last time.

On April 2, Danton found himself under arrest. Fouquier-Tinville prosecuted the Dantonists, including Desmoulins. Even Séchelles was charged with giving secrets to the enemy. The Committee of Public Safety advised the prosecution that no proof was needed against the accused. In his typically chilling manner, Saint-Just noted in the committee's letter that "the very resistance of these scoundrels proved their guilt." Danton realized soon enough what was in store. There was no defense that could save them. He raged that the prosecutors were no more than murderers. At the trial Danton proclaimed that he would "unmask the dictatorship which is now revealing itself."

Desmoulins's wife, Lucille, pleaded personally with Robespierre to spare his old friend from their student days together at the Collége de Louis-le-Grand. Robespierre refused. When Desmoulins and Danton were sentenced, Desmoulins cried out that his 23-year-old wife would also be the committee's victim. Lucille met the executioner with serene courage, as had the queen and the defiant Manon-Jean Roland, the interior minister's wife.

Before his execution, Danton predicted that Robespierre would soon follow him to the scaffold. Robespierre had a different view of the butchery his committee was carrying out throughout France. "At the point where we are now, if we stop too soon we will die." As it turned out, Robespierre perished because the Terror became unstoppable. The would-be assassin who came to his home, Cécile Rinaud, inspired by Marat's assassin, failed, but his frightened political enemies would not.

*Citizens, remember that unless justice alone rules in the Republic, freedom is a mere name. . . . Remember that there exists in your midst a swarm of rascals who are fighting against public virtue.*
—ROBESPIERRE
from his last speech

Robespierre was elected president of the National Convention in early June. The Festival of the Supreme Being on June 8 appeared to Robespierre to be his greatest triumph in his work for the Republic and the revolution. The festival's grandeur and his own utterances angered and confused both those who favored the revolutionary de-Christianization program as well as those for whom religious freedom meant nothing less than restoring the Catholic church. His own role in the spectacle and the behavior of misguided admirers harmed Robespierre's reputation. Scandal nearly engulfed the event when a woman named Cathérine Théot, a faith healer regarded as mentally unbalanced, reportedly proclaimed that Robespierre was the Messiah — the awaited Savior. The rumor was suppressed, but it infuriated many who already feared for their lives. The wily Joseph Fouché began to coordinate those who wanted to end Robespierre's Reign of Terror, which caused 60 to 80 people to die on the guillotine each day during the dreadful summer of 1794. Fouché told acquaintances that they were next on the committee's list. Though Robespierre knew about these activities, Fouché eluded capture. Saint-Just told both the Committee of Public Safety and the Committee of General Security that Robespierre had nothing to gain by establishing himself as a dictator. Finally, on July 26 (9 Thermidor), Robespierre, determined to find and crush his enemies, went before the National Convention and stated that a purge was necessary to rid the revolution of the Terror. This could be achieved only by punishing the conspirators. He himself was an innocent "slave of freedom." As he had done on numerous occasions in his career, he portrayed

**Robespierre lies on a table suffering from the gunshot wound that nearly succeeded in cheating the executioner. The Reign of Terror had turned against its prime architect.**

himself as embattled, blameless — as the revolution's defender against vice and treachery. He defended the Terror's objectives but took no responsibility for the terrible penalties it exacted. He called himself a "martyr to the Republic" and condemned those others who made the revolution "fearsome to the people," but he no longer wielded the same influence. The revolution had turned on its champion. One of those accused by Robespierre shouted, "One man alone [Robespierre] is paralyzing the will of the National Convention." Robespierre was mocked and shouted down with cries of "Down with the tyrant." Defeated, he took his seat and was arrested shortly afterward.

A scramble between forces loyal to Robespierre and those loyal to the convention followed. The Insurrectionary Paris Commune declared itself in revolt against the National Convention in protest against the arrest of Robespierre and his followers. Robespierre was taken to the Luxembourg prison, but the commune had ordered the gatekeeper to accept no new prisoners. He then was taken to the Hôtel de Ville, where, confident that he would prevail, he surrounded himself with supporters and sent notes to the commune. In the early morning hours, troops loyal to the National Convention burst into Robespierre's rooms. Gunshots were fired, and Robespierre was wounded in the jaw. Although Charles-André Merda has taken credit for shooting Robespierre, it has also been suggested that his wounds resulted from a suicide attempt.

Robespierre was carried on a stretcher to the offices of the Committee of Public Safety, where his wound was treated after many hours. He was then moved again and sentenced to death by the Revolutionary Tribunal. At 8:00 on the evening of July 28, when the bandages were ripped from his jaw by the executioner, Robespierre cried out in pain. He was then beheaded. The Terror had claimed its master. His own extreme doctrine of virtue, the constant fear of conspiracy, together with the Committee of Public Safety's efficiency, led Robespierre on a quest that ended in his destruction.

His jaw in bandages, Maximilien Robespierre prepares to follow his supporters in a final encounter with "revolutionary justice." In the end, the forces he had helped to unleash proved to be beyond Robespierre's control.

# Further Reading

Belloc, Hilaire. *Robespierre: A Study.* New York: Libraries Press, 1972.

Burke, Edmund. *Reflections on the Revolution in France.* New York: Bobbs Merrill, 1955.

Carr, John Lawrence. *Robespierre: The Force of Circumstance.* New York: St. Martin's Press, 1972.

Dwyer, Frank. *Danton.* New York: Chelsea House, 1987.

Hampson, Norman. *The Life and Opinions of Maximilien Robespierre.* London: Duckworth, 1974.

Palmer, R. R. *Twelve Who Ruled.* Princeton, NJ: Princeton University Press, 1973.

Tocqueville, Alexis de. *The Old Régime and the French Revolution.* Garden City, NY: Doubleday, 1955.

# Chronology

| | |
|---|---|
| May 6, 1758 | Born Maximilien François Marie Isidore Derobespierre in Arras, France |
| 1780 | Earns law degree at the University of Paris |
| Nov. 1781 | Begins career as a barrister in Artois province |
| March 1782 | Appointed magistrate |
| April 26, 1789 | Elected a deputy to the Third Estate of the Estates-General |
| May 5, 1789 | Estates-General convene at Versailles |
| June 17, 1789 | Third Estate adopts the title of National Assembly |
| June 20, 1789 | Robespierre signs the "tennis court oath" |
| July 14, 1789 | Mob storms the Bastille prison-fortress |
| Aug. 26, 1789 | National Assembly approves the Declaration of the Rights of Man and Citizen |
| Oct. 5–6, 1789 | Six thousand women march from Paris to Versailles; both the royal family and the National Assembly move to Paris |
| March 1790 | Robespierre becomes president of the Jacobin Club |
| June 20, 1791 | Royal family tries to escape to Varennes |
| Oct. 1, 1791 | Legislative Assembly convenes |
| April 20, 1792 | Louis XVI declares war against Austria, under Girondist pressure; War of the First Coalition begins |
| Aug. 10, 1792 | Mob storms the Tuileries in Paris; Louis XVI imprisoned |
| Sept. 20, 1792 | National Convention convenes |
| Sept. 22, 1792 | National Convention declares the French Republic |
| Jan. 14–17, 1793 | National Convention debates the fate of Louis XVI; Robespierre argues for executing the king |
| Jan. 21, 1793 | Louis XVI is guillotined |
| Feb.–March 1793 | France declares war on England, Holland, and Spain, and annexes Monaco |
| June 2, 1793 | Girondist deputies expelled from the National Convention |
| June 24, 1793 | National Convention approves a national constitution |
| July 27, 1793 | Robespierre joins the Committee of Public Safety |
| Sept. 5, 1793 | Hébertist coup attempt fails |
| Sept. 17, 1793 | Law of Suspects is passed; Reign of Terror begins, directed by Committee of Public Safety |
| Oct. 31, 1793 | Girondist leaders are guillotined |
| June 8, 1794 | Robespierre leads the Festival of the Supreme Being |
| June 10, 1794 | Sponsors the Law of the 22nd Prairial |
| July 26, 1794 | Appears before National Convention; calls for a purge of conspirators |
| July 27, 1794 | Arrested by the National Convention |
| July 28, 1794 | Maximilien Robespierre is guillotined |

# Index

**S. L. Carson** was chairman of the White House Conference on Presidential Children and is currently president of The Lincoln Group of the District of Columbia, Inc. He has written several books and his articles have appeared in numerous publications. As a professional speaker, Mr. Carson has appeared on national television and has served as speechwriter to Betty Ford, among others. He currently trains public speakers in Silver Springs, Maryland.

**Arthur M. Schlesinger, jr.,** taught history at Harvard for many years and is currently Albert Schweitzer Professor of the Humanities at City University of New York. He is the author of numerous highly praised works in American history and has twice been awarded the Pulitzer Prize. He served in the White House as special assistant to Presidents Kennedy and Johnson.